THIRD EDITION

A METHOD FOR WRITING ESSAYS ABOUT LITERATURE

THIRD EDITION

A METHOD FOR WRITING
ESSAYS ABOUT LITERATURE

PAUL HEADRICK
Langara College

TOP HAT   **NELSON**

TOP HAT

A Method for Writing Essays about Literature, Third Edition

by Paul Headrick

VP, Product and Partnership Solutions:
Anne Williams

Publisher, Digital and Print Content:
Lenore Taylor-Atkins

Executive Marketing Manager:
Amanda Henry

Content Development Manager:
Rachel Eagen

Photo and Permissions Researcher:
Sandra Mark

Production Project Manager:
Hedy Sellers

Production Service:
Cenveo Publisher Services

Copy Editor:
Elspeth McFadden

Proofreader:
Pushpa V. Giri

Indexer:
BIM Creatives, LLC

Design Director:
Ken Phipps

Managing Designer:
Franca Amore

Interior Design:
Sharon Lucas

Cover Design:
Sharon Lucas

Cover Image:
chatchaisurakram/iStockphoto

Compositor:
Cenveo Publisher Services

COPYRIGHT © 2017, 2013 by Tophatmonocle Corp.

Printed and bound in Canada
7 8 9 10 23 22 21 20

For more information contact Tophatmonocle Corp., 151 Bloor Street West, Suite 200, Toronto, Ontario, M5S 1S4. Or you can visit tophat.com

Library and Archives Canada Cataloguing in Publication Data

Headrick, Paul, author
A method for writing essays about literature / Paul Headrick (Langara College). — Third edition.

Includes bibliographical references and index.
ISBN 978-0-17-670343-1 (paperback)

1. English language—Rhetoric.
2. Literature—History and criticism—Theory, etc.
3. Criticism—Authorship.
4. Exposition (Rhetoric).
5. Report writing. I. Title.

PE1479.C7H32 2016 808'.0668
C2015-907583-1

ISBN-13: 978-0-17-670343-1
ISBN-10: 0-17-670343-8

TABLE OF CONTENTS

INTRODUCTION

For many students, literary analysis essays are a mystery. First-year students commonly want to know such things as how their essays should begin, whether they must agree with what other critics have said, and whether they should include their personal responses. *A Method for Writing Essays about Literature* answers such questions. It provides clarity by explaining the literary analysis essay's purpose and by guiding students through its structure, using exercises, examples of essay components, and sample essays.

The sample essays in Appendix 2 are a crucial component of the book. After completing each chapter of the book and answering some of the exercise questions, consider reviewing one of the essays and noting how it demonstrates the writing principles that the chapter explains. When you gain confidence, you should think about how the sample essays could be improved.

In literary studies, ideas matter, and there is an important connection between structure in an essay and analytical content—the essay's ideas. When you understand how to structure your essays, you will develop more effective analysis, and you will be more successful in your literary studies.

\\ ACKNOWLEDGMENTS

I would like to thank all my supportive students and colleagues at Langara College. I am particularly indebted to my colleague Eric Ball. I am grateful to the reviewers whose comments and suggestions improved the final content of the book. They are Sarah Banting, Mount Royal University; Tim Blackmore, Western University; Greg Chan, Kwantlen Polytechnic University; Candace Fertile, Camosun College; Peter Leonard Paolucci, York University; John Pierce, Queen's University; and J. Barbara Rose, University of Toronto. I am also grateful to the reviewers of previous editions: Anita Arvast, Georgian College; Shoshanna Ganz, Memorial University; Gwendolyn Guth, Heritage College; George C. Grinnell, University of British Columbia—Okanagan; Jason Haslam, Dalhousie University; Maria Assif, University of Toronto, Scarborough Campus; Tim Blackmore, Western University; Norah Bowman-Broz, Okanagan College; Lucille Charlton, Mount Royal University; Cecilia Martell, Kwantlen Polytechnic University; Dorothy Woodman, University of Alberta; and Liam Young, University of Alberta.

Special thanks to Heather Burt for her many contributions. I'm very grateful to Rachel Eagen and Laura Macleod of Nelson Education Ltd., and many others at Nelson who have helped with the book. Thanks to Elspeth McFadden for very wise and skilled copyediting.

\\ ABOUT THE AUTHOR

Paul Headrick has been teaching English Literature at Langara College, Vancouver, for more than twenty years. He is the author of a novel, *That Tune Clutches My Heart*, and a short story collection, *The Doctrine of Affections*. He has a Ph.D. in English from York University.

AUDIENCE AND THE LITERARY ANALYSIS ESSAY

\\ THE IMPORTANCE OF AUDIENCE

To communicate effectively, you need to know your audience. The audiences for different kinds of writing can vary a great deal. Audiences may be very literate, or they may be made up of people who are just beginning to learn to read. They may be composed of experts in your specific area, or absolute beginners, or a mixture of both. There are many other ways in which audiences differ, requiring different approaches to writing in order to be effective.

You probably already have some experience adjusting the way you write in order to respond to your sense of your audience. You would not write the same way in a note to a roommate as you would in a memo to a boss. It is also likely that you have some sound ideas about the audience for academic essays and how that audience affects the way you should write. Most students, for example, know that their readers expect a certain formality. They know that their audience is highly literate.

What makes writing effective depends on the purpose of the audience, so to write well you must understand that purpose. One of the most common pieces of advice given to writers—whether they are writing essays, newspaper stories, or novels— is to be interesting. This is good advice. What you write will have little impact if it bores readers so much that they won't read it. It may not be obvious, however, what makes something interesting to a particular audience.

Read the following sentences and consider which is the most interesting. Which one would make you want to read further?

1. "It was a bright cold day in April, and the clocks were striking thirteen" (Orwell 4).

2. One strategy works better than any other for those trying to find dancing partners in the nightclubs of Vienna.

3. Elise Partridge's poem "Farewell Desires" is a subtle plea for peace in the face of death.

4. There are three keys to writing successful literary analysis essays.

If your purpose is to find engrossing but serious entertainment, sentence 1, the first sentence of George Orwell's novel *Nineteen Eighty-Four*, might be the most interesting. If you like to dance and are planning a trip by yourself to Vienna, or if you are simply interested in Austrian culture or dancing in general, sentence 2 will probably be most interesting to you. Similarly, how interesting you find the other sentences will depend to a large degree on what your purpose is before you begin reading. If you want to know more about the meaning of Partridge's "Farewell Desires," then you are likely to be interested in sentence 3. Since you are reading this book, you probably care about writing essays about literature, in which case you might find sentence 4 the most interesting, if only for the moment.

KEY POINTS

- Writers need to know who their audience is.
- Writers need to understand and respond to the purpose of their audience.

\\ THE AUDIENCE FOR THE LITERARY ANALYSIS ESSAY

The purpose of the audience for the literary analysis essay is to explore the meaning of literary texts. Specific beliefs and expectations are connected to this purpose.

The audience believes that literature is important. In many different cultures, in many different eras, literature has commanded people's attention, and it has moved them. It is a central, vital part of most modern societies. People debate which literary texts are important and deserve our special attention, and the participants in this debate agree on the fundamental importance of literature. One way that the importance of literary study is demonstrated is by the position universities give to it. In most universities in Canada and the United States, students must complete at least one introductory course involving literary analysis in order to obtain a bachelor's degree, whether in the arts or the sciences, and often even in professional programs such as nursing and engineering. The bachelor's degree, no matter what the discipline, signifies a certain range of under-standing of ourselves and our world; the common requirement that literary study be part of the undergraduate degree demonstrates its widely accepted importance.

The audience for the literary analysis essay also believes that literature is compli-cated. We want to understand the things that are important to us. At the same time that literature feels important, its complexity makes it mysterious. Its meanings are expressed indirectly. These meanings are subtle, sometimes contradictory, even changing. The combination of literature's importance and its complexity is what makes it worth reading, rereading, and studying—both for you and your audience. Concentrating on your audi-ence's purpose—to explore that complexity in your writing—will help you to focus your essays effectively.

More needs to be said, however, about the audience's interest in the meaning of literary texts. Here are some key ideas about your audience. Each point has important consequences for you as you write your essay:

1. The audience for your essay believes that literary texts can be poems, plays, stories, and novels, but literary texts may also include films, graphic novels, and other texts that communicate with images or sounds.

   Consequence: The analytical techniques that apply to texts traditionally thought of as literary also apply to texts that have elements other than words.

2. The audience for your essay has already read (or viewed) the literary text you are writing about, and, on at least a simple level, has understood it.

   Consequence: Your audience will not be interested in summaries of **plots**, descriptions of **settings**, lists of **characters**,[1] paraphrases of conversations, and so on. Your audience knows these things already.

3. The audience for your essay believes that literary texts express important ideas in subtle and complicated ways.

   Consequence: Your audience accepts the idea that there is much more to say about a literary text than what is contained in a summary. Your audience expects your essay to deal with features of the text that are not obvious.

4. The audience for your essay wants to know more about the ideas of the literary text you are writing about and also wants to know more about how those ideas are expressed.

   Consequence: You do not have to establish how good or interesting the literary text is. Your essay should focus on an idea expressed by the literary text.

5. The audience for your essay believes that not only the main features of a text but also its smallest details are potentially important and meaningful.

   Consequence: In order for your analysis to be convincing, you should be prepared to consider details such as word choice, the arrangement of words on the page, or individual images.

6. The audience for your essay believes that the complexity of literary texts generates different meanings, and that these meanings can change when texts are read in different historical contexts.

---

[1] For brief definitions of bolded literary terms and some advice on how to use them in your analyses, see Appendix 5: Glossary of Literary Terms.

Consequence: There is always more to be said about literary texts. You do not need to worry that because several essays have already been written about a particular text, your audience will be uninterested in reading yet another analysis.

7. The audience for your essay believes that differing views about a literary text can be legitimate.

   Consequence: You do not need to worry about what the "right" interpretation of a text is and whether your analysis agrees with it.

8. The audience for your essay believes that although differing views about a literary text can be legitimate, your interpretation does not merit serious consideration just because you believe it.

   Consequence: Your audience will not be interested in an interpretation that is based simply on what you "feel" is the text's meaning. Your interpretation must be *convincing*. You must prove that your interpretation makes sense, supporting your claims with evidence and analysis.

9. The audience for your essay is highly literate.

   Consequence: The language of your literary analysis essay must be technically correct, clear, and effective. Your audience will not be impressed by artificially difficult vocabulary or needlessly complex sentences, but it will expect your essay to use **abstract** language and terms specific to literary analysis with a high degree of precision.

There is an important sense in which there is another, separate audience for your literary analysis essay—the instructor who is marking your assignment. Your instructor will be evaluating your essay in part by considering how well it demonstrates an under-standing of its hypothetical audience, but you should keep a few points in mind regarding your instructor specifically.

1. Your instructor believes that an understanding of key concepts of literary analysis introduced in the course contributes to successful interpretations of texts.

   Consequence: You should make careful note when new ideas are introduced in your course, whether they have to do with the specific literary texts you are dis-cussing or literature in general. In an introductory course, for instance, you might hear a lecture that includes a definition of a literary device and shows its impor-tance in a text. You should be alert to instances where the same device appears in the text you are analyzing, and you should demonstrate that you have mastered the concept by including it as evidence in your essay.

2. Your instructor knows that you are a student.

   Consequence: You do not need to worry about whether your essay is absolutely original or whether you understand everything that is relevant to the text you are analyzing. The level of understanding that your essay demonstrates will be evaluated appropriately for the level of study at which you are working. Students sometimes begin English literature courses with the sense that they are terrible at literary analysis. You should be confident that your classmates share your sense that you are engaged in something difficult; it is your instructor's job is to introduce you to techniques for beginning to deal with that difficulty. Do not worry if the analysis you produce seems less sophisticated than that of the literary critics you read.

3. Your instructor values clarity.

   Consequence: Be clear. Your instructor has an obligation to read your essay carefully, but you should not think that this obligation makes clarity any less important. When composing the final draft of your essay, imagine that your instructor will be marking it after having already read twenty such essays and with twenty more still to go. Work hard to be clear so that your ideas stand out and get the credit they deserve.

   If you think further about the audience for the essay and what the audience is interested in, you can come up with examples of statements that will be off topic and uninteresting, such as statements about how important the story is to your life or how relevant the story is to issues in the world. Such statements are perfectly appropriate in a different context, but they are out of place in a literary analysis essay written for an audience with a focused interest in the meaning of a literary text.

KEY POINTS

- The audience for literary analysis essays wants to know about the meaning of literary texts.

- The audience for literary analysis essays believes that literature is complicated and important.

- The specific expectations of the audience have important consequences for the content of literary analysis essays.

EXERCISE SET 1.1—UNDERSTANDING AUDIENCE

In Exercises 1.1 A and 1.1 B, indicate whether each sentence would provoke the specific interest of the audience for a literary analysis essay. (Note that the full text of the poem "Farewell Desires" is included at the end of Chapter 2.)

Exercise 1.1 A (Answers are in Appendix 4)

1. Elise Partridge's poem "Farewell Desires" made me cry.
2. "Farewell Desires" is one of Elise Partridge's best poems.
3. The **speaker** of Elise Partridge's poem "Farewell Desires" imagines crossing over a drawbridge.
4. "Farewell Desires," by Elise Partridge, presents the author's true feelings about death.
5. In Elise Partridge's "Farewell Desires," the speaker connects enlightenment to dispensing with worldly desire.

Exercise 1.1 B

1. Protecting the environment is one of the most important issues that all humanity must face.
2. In "Farewell Desires," the speaker's attitude to death develops with a series of similes.
3. The imagery in Elise Partridge's "Farewell Desires" subtly conveys the speaker's wish for a shift in her feelings about death to come as part of a natural process.
4. In person, the poet Elise Partridge was generous and unpretentious.
5. The best of the five verse paragraphs of Elise Partridge's "Farewell Desires" is the last.

Exercise 1.1 C

1. Write three different statements that refer to a literary text you are studying in class but that do not respond to the interests of the audience for a literary analysis essay. Give a brief explanation of why each statement would be uninteresting to such an audience.

CHAPTER 2
ANALYTICAL PARAGRAPHS

The analytical paragraph is the heart of the literary analysis essay. It develops a single idea about part of a literary text, supporting that idea with evidence (usually, but not always, in the form of quotations) and analysis. A sequence of analytical paragraphs in a literary analysis essay forms a logical argument in support of a thesis. In English literature (and in most disciplines in the humanities and social sciences), what matters most in an essay is analytical content. Properly structuring analytical paragraphs will not ensure that your analysis is insightful, imaginative, and convincing, but it will lead you to develop your analysis and to present it effectively.

\\ INITIAL ANALYSIS

Begin by reading carefully, and then rereading. The description of the paragraph structure presented in this chapter is not a description of the writing process, but we will touch on that process here. When beginning to write, do not feel that the first thing you must produce is an insightful analytical claim, followed by correctly presented evidence, and so on. Read and reread the literary text you are studying. Make notes about those features of the text that are particularly difficult or intriguing. Identify any of the elements of literature you have been studying in class, from **rhyme** schemes to **symbols**.[1] Note your observations on what the text is suggesting about certain characters, what issues are being raised, or the significance of any evidence that strikes you as important. If the text is quite short, you might even want to complete a close reading as a first step (see Chapter 5).

 Be ready to make discoveries. Once you begin writing an analytical paragraph, you may find that ideas will occur to you that are different from what you have stated in your claim. Simply adjust your claim to reflect your discovery. Worry about key-word repetition and other techniques for creating clarity in your analysis only after you have written some of your ideas down, rather than struggling to get the paragraph exactly right with your first draft.

---

[1] For brief definitions of bolded literary terms and some advice on how to use them in your analyses, see Appendix 5: Glossary of Literary Terms.

As you become more experienced in writing effectively structured analytical paragraphs, you will find that you read literary texts more effectively, seeing more evidence that needs to be analyzed and developing better ideas about what the evidence suggests.

\\ ANALYTICAL PARAGRAPHS AND THEIR THREE COMPONENTS

Analytical paragraphs have three components: the claim, the evidence, and the analysis. The claim is a specific kind of topic sentence that begins each analytical paragraph and makes the point that the paragraph will try to demonstrate. The evidence is the material from the text that supports the claim. The analysis explains how the evidence supports the claim.

Everything in an analytical paragraph should be identifiable as claim, evidence, or analysis. If a sentence or phrase is not one of these things, it does not belong in the paragraph.

CLAIMS
Defining and Understanding Claims

The claim states what the paragraph is going to prove. It is the topic sentence, the first sentence of the paragraph. You can think of the claim as the "thesis" of the paragraph, and, in fact, it needs to be connected to the thesis of your essay. (The way your essay makes this connection is discussed in Chapter 3.) The claim is very important, as the analysis is unlikely to be successful without a good claim.

An effective analytical claim makes a point about something significant that is suggested or indirectly revealed by the text you are analyzing. Remember, as always, that your audience has read the text and has understood it on a simple level. The claim must go beyond the obvious and lead to an analysis of something communicated indirectly.

Consider the following potential claims, each of which refers to the description of the husband in the opening paragraphs of Charlotte Perkins Gilman's short story "The Yellow Wallpaper" (see Appendix 3):

1. The **narrator's** husband, John, discourages his wife from speculating about the house that they have rented.

2. The narrator's husband, John, is very practical.

3. The narrator's husband, John, is confident that there is nothing really wrong with his wife.

The problem is that each sentence presents what amounts to a paraphrase or summary of part of the story. Students frequently write sentences like these when making their first attempts to compose claims. Each of the statements can be shown to be true, and it may be that a fear of being incorrect contributes to the problem.

Because each statement is a paraphrase or summary, each will fail to lead to analysis. One of the signs that sentence 1 is weak is that its main verb, "discourages," refers to something the character does, rather than the significance of what he does. The sentence is likely to lead to a simple presentation of a fact, with very little analysis needed. Sentence 2 has the same problem. The narrator says that John is "practical." The sentence simply repeats a fact presented directly in the story. Sentence 3 is a little bit better, but not much. The narrator does not use the word "confident" when describing how John feels about his diagnosis. She does, however, point out that he shares what he thinks with everyone else. A reasonable reader would see, on first reading, that John is confident about what he believes.

It is not always possible to know whether a claim is analytical without having read the text to which it refers. We can imagine a context in which a statement like sentence 3 might, in fact, be an analytical claim. If the story we are writing about presents a character whose confidence is conveyed indirectly, in such a way that it might be overlooked by a reasonable reader, then a statement asserting that the character is confident is useful, with support from evidence and substantial analysis.

Avoid claims that state what characters do. Such claims usually lead to summaries of characters' actions and are not really claims at all. Make certain that your claims about characters, objects, words, images, or any features of the analyzed texts are not just summaries of what a reasonable reader would find obvious.

Use verbs in your claims that will tend to lead to analysis. Useful verbs include "suggests," "implies," "reveals," "represents," and "symbolizes." These verbs will not guarantee that you have an effective claim, but they will make it more likely. They may also make it clearer to you that your claim has a problem and needs revision. For example, if you were to write, "The narrator's description of her husband suggests that he is very practical," and then quote the line in which she states that he is "practical in the extreme," it should be clear to you that his practicality is not "suggested" but is asserted directly.

The earlier statements could be revised to create more effective claims that identify ideas that the text communicates more indirectly. Consider the following sentences:

1. John's response to his wife's feelings about the house suggests that he does not respect her imagination.

2. John's confidence that his wife is not really ill reveals that he lacks empathy.

3. The various ways in which the story emphasizes John's practicality suggest that he represents rationality.

Each of these claims is more effective than those in the previous list. In each case, the claim has been revised by considering the further meaning of the evidence.

Note that although the audience wants to know about the meaning of the literary text, the claims do not have to address this question directly. (The thesis, which will be discussed in Chapter 3, must do so.) The audience understands that a series of claims about what is communicated indirectly by certain evidence in the literary text will form an argument that will, eventually, address the story's meaning. Each claim must be about the story or some part of the story, and each claim must not simply summarize, but state something about what is communicated indirectly.

KEY POINTS

- The claim begins the paragraph and states what the paragraph will prove.
- The claim makes a point about something suggested or revealed indirectly by the text.
- Avoid claims that state what characters do.

EXERCISE SET 2.1—IDENTIFYING CLAIMS

Exercises 2.1 A and 2.1 B present some examples of potential claims. They refer to Charlotte Perkins Gilman's short story "The Yellow Wallpaper" (see Appendix 3). For each case, indicate whether or not you think the claim is analytical. Sometimes it is not easy to tell whether a statement is an analytical claim without knowing more about the text. The statement that a character is angry may be an obvious report of a fact about one character, who, for example, says that she is angry; on the other hand, it may take analysis to support such a statement about another character, whose feelings are only revealed indirectly. Even if you do not read "The Yellow Wallpaper," however, you should be able to make an educated guess about whether the following sentences are potential claims—statements that will lead to analysis—or not.

Exercise 2.1 A (Answers are in Appendix 4)

1. The narrator of the story is isolated in a room of the house.
2. The description of the room in which the narrator is isolated suggests that she is actually in prison.
3. The narrator's sister-in-law helps to keep her isolated.
4. The narrator's sister-in-law represents the forces that oppress the narrator.
5. The descriptions of the wallpaper reveal the narrator's inner life.

Exercise 2.1 B

1. The wallpaper confuses and disgusts the narrator.
2. The narrator's response to the wallpaper suggests that she is confused about her identity.

---

3. A pattern of similes in the story establishes the narrator's negative feelings about rationality.

4. The narrator uses many similes.

5. The narrator is frustrated by her husband.

Exercise 2.1 C

1. Write a claim that identifies something revealed indirectly about a character in a literary text that you have been discussing in class.

2. Write a claim that identifies something revealed indirectly about the world that is described by a literary text that you have been discussing in class.

EVIDENCE
Defining and Understanding Evidence

Evidence is information that supports the claim. The evidence is usually in the form of quotations, but it can also be paraphrase and summary, especially in the case of visual texts, such as illustrations from graphic novels. (Integrating Quotations from Literary Texts, pages 20–23, presents detailed instructions on how to include quotations in your paragraphs.) The evidence follows the claim.

Quote only those passages that you will analyze. Needlessly long quotations are confusing. The reader needs to understand how the quoted material works as evidence—how the quotation supports the claim—and if you do not discuss the material you quote, the reader will not understand the purpose of the quotation.

Separate the evidence from the claim and the analysis. Do not begin your analysis before you present the evidence, and do not include analysis at the end of the sentence that presents the evidence. It is possible to combine evidence and analysis, but doing so frequently produces awkward sentences. It also tends to shorten the analysis. Leave the analysis for separate sentences that follow the evidence.

KEY POINTS

- Evidence supports the claim.
- Quote only evidence that you analyze.
- Keep evidence separate from the claim and the analysis.

EXERCISE SET 2.2—PRESENTING EVIDENCE

Exercises 2.2 A and 2.2 B present quotations from "The Yellow Wallpaper." Indicate whether or not each sentence would be appropriate following an analytical claim. If the sentence is inappropriate in some way, explain why.

Exercise 2.2 A (Answers are in Appendix 4)

1. The narrator says that her husband "has no patience with faith, an intense horror of superstition, and he scoffs openly at any talk of things not to be felt and seen and put down in figures" (130).

2. The narrator shows that her husband is opposed to her imagination and that he represents rationality and science when she says that he "has no patience with faith, an intense horror of superstition, and he scoffs openly at any talk of things not to be felt and seen and put down in figures" (130).

3. The narrator says that her husband "has no patience with faith, an intense horror of superstition, and he scoffs openly at any talk of things not to be felt and seen and put down in figures," showing that he represents rationality and science (130).

Exercise 2.2 B

1. The narrator's report of her husband's response to her request to change rooms shows his lack of respect for women: "then he took me in his arms and called me a blessed little goose" (132).

2. The narrator describes her husband's response to her request to change rooms: "then he took me in his arms and called me a blessed little goose" (132).

3. After her request to move, the narrator reports that her husband takes her "in his arms" and calls her a "blessed little goose," revealing that he does not respect her or women in general (132).

Exercise 2.2 C

1. Write a single sentence that presents evidence to support the claim you made in Exercise 2.1 C, question 1.

2. Write a single sentence that presents evidence to support the claim you made in Exercise 2.1 C, question 2.

ANALYSIS
Defining and Understanding Analysis

The analysis explains how the evidence supports the claim. It follows the evidence, and it is most often the longest section of the paragraph. It is not enough merely to assert that the evidence reveals something. You need to show how it does so. Writers frequently overestimate how clearly and fully they have explained the connection between evidence and analysis, and the result is an unconvincing argument. If you have an insightful claim and you have selected appropriate evidence, you will need extensive analysis. If the evidence does not need to be explained, then your claim is identifying something in the literary text that is obvious—it is not really a claim at all.

The analysis should repeat key terms from the claim. The connection between the analysis and the claim needs to be very clear, and the best way to establish this clarity is through key-term repetition. If your claim states that the main character's comments about her hometown show that she is "alienated from her culture," do not state in your analysis that the evidence shows that she is "estranged from her society." It may be clear to you that the meaning of "estranged" is exactly the same as "alienated," but a change in wording risks confusing the reader, especially in a complicated essay with many abstract terms. Repeat, in some form, the key terms "alienated" and "culture."

The analysis should develop the claim. An analysis that merely repeats the claim is not sufficient. The key terms should be repeated in sentences that develop the claim further. New terms can be introduced in the analysis, but their connections to the key term, and to the claim, must be clear. If, for example, your claim states something about capitalism, your analysis might use the term "commodification," but it should be clear that what you are discussing is a feature of capitalism.

The analysis needs to refer directly to the evidence. Make sure that the analysis does not elaborate on the claim without mentioning, specifically, what part of the evidence it is addressing. If your evidence includes a fairly long quotation, you may find that it is appropriate to "requote"—that is, to include in the analysis a very short phrase or even a single word from the original quotation—in order to focus your analysis on that word or phrase. Frequently your analysis can refer back to the entire quotation, and in such cases you can refer to the evidence with a phrase that briefly summarizes it either very generally, such as "this statement," or more specifically, such as "the narrator's expression of embarrassment." You may also refer to a specific part of the evidence with phrases such as "the **caesura** in the second line" or "the first simile."

Note that the word "this" alone is not an adequate way to refer to the evidence. Generally, in academic writing, a noun or noun phrase should follow the word "this" to clarify what "this" refers to. When you refer back to the quotation, consider whether the passage is a description, a conversation, a question, or something else: hence, "this description," "this conversation," "this question." Do not say "this quotation" unless the person whose words you are quoting is quoting someone else. In all cases, you must include a phrase to make your reference to the evidence clear and direct.

The Structure of Evidence and Analysis

Two different structures can be used to present analysis immediately after evidence; these two structures are diagrammed in Figure 2.1. In Structure 1, all of the evidence is presented immediately after the analytical claim, with all of the analysis following it. In Structure 2, one bit of evidence is presented following the claim, with the analysis of that bit coming immediately after, then another bit of evidence, then more analysis, and so on. Structure 2 may appear to produce a longer paragraph, but the appearance is misleading. There may be as much evidence in the single evidence section in Structure 1 as there is in the two (or three or four) sections in Structure 2. Note that the analysis is almost always longer than the evidence.

FIGURE 2.1 \\
TWO STRUCTURES FOR THE ANALYTICAL PARAGRAPH

Structure 1	Structure 2
Claim	Claim
Evidence	Evidence
Analysis	Analysis
	Evidence
	Analysis

In some cases, either structure will work well. If the paragraph has many short quotations, all contributing to a similar point, Structure 1 is probably the most effective. If your claim has two or more distinct parts, or if the evidence is in two or more large chunks, Structure 2 is probably the most effective.

KEY POINTS

- Analysis explains how the evidence supports the claim.
- Repeat key terms from the claim.
- Develop the claim.
- Refer directly to the evidence.

\\ COMMON PROBLEMS IN ANALYTICAL PARAGRAPHS

AWKWARD REPETITION

Weak claims lead to awkward repetition. The following paragraph is an extreme example of the problem. For the sake of clarity, it has one sentence for the analytical claim, one sentence of evidence, and one sentence of analysis.

> The story reveals that Paul is very tall. The narrator says, "Paul is very tall" (17). The narrator's observation shows that Paul is very tall.

The problem in this paragraph has to do with the analytical claim, which is not a claim at all but rather a statement of fact. Because the topic sentence is a statement of fact, the evidence and analysis can only repeat the fact; there is nothing really to prove.

In order to eliminate the awkward repetition, the claim needs to state something about the *significance* of Paul's height. Here is an improved version of the paragraph:

> Paul's height symbolizes his power. The narrator says that when the group goes to the demonstration, "Paul was able to see over the crowd and describe to his friends what was going on, even though they stood at the back" (17). Later, when Jerry defers to Paul on the question of what movie to see, the narrator observes that "Paul stood up and stretched to his full height while leafing through the newspaper to choose a film" (18). The description of the crowd scene shows that Paul's height gives him power in a concrete way, for he has the power to see, physically, what his friends cannot. Jerry's deference and Paul's response to it accentuate his power even further, showing that it has a psychological component. This emphasis on Paul's height establishes it as a symbol of his power.

This paragraph is much better, mainly because it has a much more effective claim. The claim requires a more careful selection of evidence and more thorough analysis.

If your attempts at analytical paragraphs produce awkward repetition, reconsider the claim. Make sure that the claim is analytical and that it does not just state a fact.

CONFUSION ABOUT WHAT MAKES MEANING

Be clear that meaning comes from the text. Sometimes students encounter difficulty, both in the structure of their sentences and the substance of their analysis, as a consequence of confusion about what creates meaning. The three main possibilities are the author, the reader, and the text. Consider the following examples:

1. The author uses a metaphor in the third line of the poem to show that love is all-powerful.

2. From the metaphor in the third line of the poem, the reader understands that love is all-powerful.

3. The metaphor in the third line of the poem suggests that love is all-powerful.

Example 1 suggests that meaning comes from the author, an idea that makes a certain sense. Readers are sometimes asked, "What does the author mean?" as a way to get them to begin interpreting texts. Locating meaning with the author, however, frequently leads to wordiness. Making the author the source of meaning also distracts from the main focus of the literary critic's interest, which is the text, not the mind or psychology of the author. Avoid locating meaning with the author.

Example 2 suggests that meaning comes from the reader. Some interesting literary theories do, in fact, examine how readers generate meaning, but for most purposes, this approach generates wordiness and frequently produces awkward sentences. It also risks making an analysis less convincing; if you state that the reader understands something, but the reader of your essay has come to a different understanding, you, and not the reader, are obviously the one in the wrong. Avoid locating meaning with the reader.

Example 3 suggests that meaning comes from the text. This approach is less wordy, usually produces more graceful sentences, and does not risk distracting the reader from the text or failing to convince because of a logical error. Readers of your essay might disagree with you, but their disagreement alone will not constitute any sort of proof that you are wrong. If they understand the nature of literary criticism, they will read on to discover the reasons for your interpretation.

KEY POINTS

- If your paragraph is awkwardly repetitive, you need to revise the claim.
- The text creates meaning, not the reader or the author.

\\ WORKING WITH ANALYTICAL PARAGRAPHS

A SAMPLE ANALYTICAL PARAGRAPH

The following is an analytical paragraph that examines part of Charlotte Perkins Gilman's story "The Yellow Wallpaper." It would follow a paragraph that establishes that the narrator's husband thinks of her as a child.

> The narrator's reaction to the room in which she is staying suggests that she has been affected by her husband's attitude toward her, but she resists that attitude. She guesses at the history of the room: "It was nursery first and then playroom and gymnasium, I should judge; for the windows are barred for little children, and there are rings and things in the walls" (131). She also notes that the wallpaper has been stripped from portions of the walls, that the floor has been "scratched and gouged and splintered" (134), and that the bed, it seems, has been nailed down (134). These descriptions suggest a high degree of security and also desperation in the room's former occupants. They hint that the room was likelier to have been an asylum of some sort than a nursery, especially given the narrator's earlier observation that the house is isolated and its grounds carefully secured (130–31). The narrator's sense that the room was used for children, therefore, shows that she has been affected by her husband's attitude, and expects that the place she will be assigned will be that of a child. At the same

time, however, she says, "I don't like our room a bit" (131). Her resistance to the room shows that she resists her husband's effort to reduce her to a child.

EXERCISE SET 2.3—UNDERSTANDING ANALYTICAL PARAGRAPHS

Exercise 2.3 A (Answers are in Appendix 4)

1. Mark the points in the sample paragraph that separate the analytical claim, evidence, and analysis.
2. Number in order each piece of evidence that is presented.
3. Find the analysis for each piece of evidence. Give the analysis the same number as the corresponding evidence.
4. Does the order in which the analysis is presented correspond to the order in which the evidence is presented?
5. What key terms from the analytical claim are repeated in the analysis?
6. Identify the phrases in the analysis that refer directly to the evidence.
7. Does the paragraph use Structure 1 or Structure 2?

Exercise 2.3 B

1. Answer the questions in Exercise 2.3 A, applying them to the following paragraph (the second body paragraph of the essay "Freedom and Attachment in 'The Guest' by Albert Camus," which is the first sample essay in Appendix 2):

> In his relationship with the Arab prisoner, Daru experiences a **conflict** between individual freedom and attachment to another. As the story's ironic title suggests, Daru treats the man not as a prisoner but as a "guest": he feeds him, offers him a bed, and sleeps near him unarmed. His hospitality implies that Daru feels responsible for the man's well-being. Yet when the man asks, "Why do you eat with me?" Daru replies, "I'm hungry" (216). Daru's response suggests that despite his feeling of responsibility, he resists the idea of a relationship with the man. Rather than offering an explanation that has something to do with the man, Daru focuses on himself and his own hunger. The tension between freedom and attachment is also evident when Daru sends the prisoner off with food and money and directions to both the police station and the shelter of the nomads. By providing the man with basic necessities, Daru implicitly acknowledges his attachment to him. His refusal to advise the man, however, suggests a desire to remain free from attachments or responsibilities to another.

EXERCISE SET 2.4—CREATING ANALYTICAL PARAGRAPHS

In Exercises 2.4 A and 2.4 B, follow the instructions to complete the analytical paragraphs.

Exercise 2.4 A (Answers are in Appendix 4)

1. The following paragraph, on the story "The Yellow Wallpaper," has an analytical claim, followed by evidence, but no analysis. Complete the paragraph by adding several sentences that analyze the evidence and show how the evidence supports the claim. Be sure to refer directly to the evidence.

> The narrator's initial description of the wallpaper suggests her own mental fragility as well as her unconscious sense that she is threatened by something evil:
>
> > It is dull enough to confuse the eye in the following, pronounced enough to constantly irritate and provoke study, and when you follow the lame uncertain curves for a little distance they suddenly commit suicide—plunge off at outrageous angles, destroy themselves in unheard of contradictions.
> >
> > The color is repellent, almost revolting; a smouldering unclean yellow, strangely faded by the slow-turning sunlight.
> >
> > It is a dull yet lurid orange in some places, a sickly sulphur tint in others. (134)

2. The following paragraph, on the poem "Farewell Desires," has evidence, followed by analysis, but it is missing the analytical claim. (The full poem can be found at the end of this chapter.) Complete the paragraph by adding a single sentence at the beginning, making a claim that is consistent with the analysis that follows:

> In the first verse paragraph the speaker imagines freeing herself from what she describes as "desires' pinioning buckles" (line 2). Implicitly, the phrase personifies desire, for only a person can fasten buckles. The word "pinioning" connotes a certain deliberation and even cruelty, suggesting that desire, rather than being an aspect of her self, is something independent of and hostile to her, leaving her imprisoned and helpless. In the final verse paragraph the speaker calls on the "Goddess of discards" to help her overcome desire (17). This invocation personifies whatever power it is that opposes desire, which, as in the case of desire itself, suggests it is a force that is independent of the speaker. Identifying this force as a "goddess" implies it is good, even worthy of worship, and by calling on the goddess the speaker's plea becomes a kind of prayer.

Exercise 2.4 B

1. The following paragraph, on the poem "Farewell Desires," has an analytical claim, followed by evidence, but no analysis. Complete the paragraph by

adding several sentences that analyze the evidence and show how it supports the claim. Be sure to refer directly to the evidence.

A series of images suggests that to be without desire is also to abandon a kind of control of one's existence. The speaker says that to be free from desire is "to bob away, an untethered dory / from a golden shore" (3–4), "To be tumbled by whim / bloom to bloom to bloom" (5–6), and, finally, in asking to be without desire, she imagines herself "a water-fall / pouring a heedless mile" (18–19).

2. The following paragraph, on the story "The Yellow Wallpaper," has evidence, followed by analysis, but it is missing the analytical claim. Complete the paragraph by adding a single sentence at the beginning, making a claim that is consistent with the analysis that follows.

Soon after the narrator and her husband move into the house, she tells him, on what she describes as a "moonlight evening," that there is something strange about the place (131). Weeks later, before making another attempt to tell him of her feelings, she again notices the moon:

It was moonlight. The moon shines in all around   just as the sun does.

I hate to see it sometimes, it creeps so slowly, and always comes in by one window or another.

John was asleep and I hated to waken him, so I kept still and watched the moonlight on that undulating wall-paper till I felt creepy. (136)

The narrator says that at night, "worst of all by moonlight," she notices that the pattern on the wallpaper "becomes bars," and "the woman behind it as plain as can be" (138). Finally, as the story approaches its climax, the narrator says, "As soon as it was moonlight and that poor thing began to crawl and shake the pattern, I got up and ran to help her" (141). The moon is a public symbol of the feminine, and the narrator's negative comments about it, hating to see it, feeling "creepy" when she watches it, finding the clarity with which it reveals the bars and the woman behind them to be "worst of all," suggest that she has internalized her society's misogyny. She is almost sickened by the moon, and, the text suggests, sickened by the fact that she is a woman. At the same time, how-ever, the presence of the moon, and the way the way the moon asserts the power of the feminine, gives her power. She finds the power to acknowl-edge her feelings and challenge patriarchy, represented by her husband, when the moon shines. It is in moonlight that she sees the woman behind the bars clearly, and, symbolically, sees that she is imprisoned by patriarchy. She makes her bid to free the woman, and, thus, herself, again when the moon shines, suggesting that power and freedom can only come by overcoming her internalized misogyny and basing her identity on the feminine.

Exercise 2.4 C

1. Add several sentences of analysis to follow the evidence you presented in Exercise 2.2 C, question 1.

2. Add several sentences of analysis to follow the evidence you presented in Exercise 2.2 C, question 2.

3. In each of your answers above, identify the phrases that refer directly to the evidence.

4. In each of your answers above, identify the words that repeat key terms from the claims.

\\ INTEGRATING QUOTATIONS FROM LITERARY TEXTS

The evidence essential to literary analysis essays comes from literary texts. Most often, the evidence is presented in the form of quotations. In order to make convincing arguments about texts, you need to show exactly how those texts do what you state they do by presenting parts of the text as evidence and analyzing that evidence thoroughly. It is important that you integrate quotations into your essay effectively.

GUIDELINES FOR INTEGRATING QUOTATIONS

1. **The quotation must be part of one of your own sentences.** If the quotation simply appears in your essay, unconnected to your own thought, it is not clear what its function is in your argument.

   Incorrect: The narrator admits that her feelings for her husband are changing. "The fact is I am getting a little afraid of John" (138).

   Correct: The narrator admits that her feelings for her husband are changing: "The fact is I am getting a little afraid of John" (138).

   Correct: The narrator says that she is "getting a little afraid" of her husband (138).

   Note that in the first correct example, the only change that is made is the substitution of the colon for the period. The colon makes the quotation part of the larger sentence and establishes that the quotation is the specific example of what is stated generally in the first part of the sentence.

2. **Identify whose words are being quoted.** The words you quote are always spoken or written by someone, and who is responsible for the words makes a difference, sometimes a very great difference, to the significance of those words. You must, therefore, make it clear whose words are being quoted. This requirement holds even if the words are those of a third-person narrator of a story or the **speaker** of a poem. Narrators and speakers are fictional creations, and what they say or think is frequently in no way equivalent to what the text as a whole suggests.

Incorrect: The narrator's husband "is practical in the extreme" (130).

Correct: The narrator says that her husband "is practical in the extreme" (130).

The significance of the description of the narrator's husband is connected to who is doing the describing. It suggests something about a quality in her husband, but it also suggests something of her awareness of that quality, and, subtly, a lack of complete respect for it.

3. **Include important information about the quotation.** The meaning of the quotation is not only connected to who is speaking but also to the position of the quotation in the literary text. Enough information must be presented for the reader to understand what the quotation refers to and to situate it in relation to the rest of the text.

Incorrect: The speaker imagines herself "pouring a heedless mile" (19).

Correct: In the final verse paragraph, the speaker prays to become "a waterfall / pouring a heedless mile" (18–19).

In the first example, we do not know that the speaker is asking to become a waterfall, so we cannot really analyze the image. In the second example, we know that this prayer comes at the end of the poem, which in itself is important, and we have a clearer understanding of what she is praying for.

4. **Refer to the quotation in the present tense.**

Incorrect: The narrator exclaimed, "I think that woman gets out in the daytime!" (140).

Correct: The narrator exclaims, "I think that woman gets out in the daytime!" (140).

We assume that the things that happen in a literary text are always happening, in a kind of "literary present." Using the past tense suggests that the text or events in the text are over in a way that makes sense in real life but not when discussing texts that are "re-created" every time someone reads them. Use words that establish sequences in time, such as "earlier" or "before," rather than shifts in tense to indicate when one event takes place before another.

Incorrect:	The narrator refers to the puzzle of the wallpaper and says, "I don't want to leave now until I have found it out" (138). Earlier, she was anxious to leave.
Correct:	The narrator refers to the puzzle of the wallpaper and says, "I don't want to leave now until I have found it out" (138). Earlier, she is anxious to leave.

Though the past tense ("was") would be correct if the sentence referred to something in real life, the present tense ("is") is correct when referring to a literary event.

5. **Refer to the entire quotation.** It is confusing if the content of the quotation is different from what the introductory phrase states it will be.

Incorrect:	The narrator describes the size of his house: "It's huge, and it makes me lonely."
Correct:	The narrator comments on his house and how it makes him feel: "It's huge, and it makes me lonely."
Correct:	The narrator says that his house is "huge" and that it makes him feel "lonely."

6. **Use an accurate and informative verb to refer to the quotation.**

Incorrect:	The narrator explains, "I cry at nothing, and cry most of the time (134).
Correct:	The narrator admits, "I cry at nothing, and cry most of the time (134).

Note that the word "describes" cannot be used as a synonym for "says."

Incorrect:	The narrator describes that "the house is red" (29).
Correct:	The narrator says that "the house is red" (29).

7. **Apply the rules of grammar and syntax to sentences that include quotations.**

Incorrect:	The speaker says, "and magpie curios" (11).
Correct:	The speaker says she wants to get rid of the "magpie curios" accumulated by the "devil of hoarding" (29).

8. **Include in your analysis a noun or noun phrase that refers directly to the quotation.**
   The phrase is needed in order to make clear to the reader what the analysis is based on.

   Incorrect: John says to the narrator, "'Bless her little heart!'" (137). He is condescending.

   Correct: John says to the narrator, "'Bless her little heart!'" (137). His expression of approval reveals his condescension.

9. **Do not use a quotation as the subject of a sentence.**

   Incorrect: "To unwind yourself like Houdini" shows that the speaker regards being without desire as a difficult goal (3).

   Correct: The speaker says that she hopes to escape from desire's "pinioning buckles" (2) like "Houdini" (3). The image shows that she regards being without desire as an almost impossibly difficult goal.

EXERCISE SET 2.5—INTEGRATING QUOTATIONS

Exercise 2.5 A (Answers are in Appendix 4)

The following questions refer to the sample analytical paragraph on "The Yellow Wallpaper" on page 16.

1. How many quotations in the paragraph stand as sentences on their own, rather than being part of larger sentences?
2. In what tense are the events of the story presented?
3. Identify the words or phrases that specify whose words are being quoted.
4. Identify the one case in which an independent clause introduces a quotation.
5. What punctuation mark follows the independent clause that introduces a quotation?

Exercise 2.5 B

The following questions refer to the sample analytical paragraph on "The Guest" on page 17.

1. How many quotations in the paragraph stand as sentences on their own, rather than being part of larger sentences?
2. In what tense are the events of the story presented?
3. Identify the words or phrases that identify whose words are being quoted.

Exercise 2.5 C

1. Review your answer to Exercise 2.4 C, question 1. Using the Guidelines for Integrating Quotations above, correct any errors.
2. Review your answer to Exercise 2.4 C, question 2. Using the Guidelines for Integrating Quotations above, correct any errors.

FAREWELL DESIRES

To unwind yourself like Houdini
from desires' pinioning buckles,
to bob away, an untethered dory
from a golden shore.

To be tumbled by whim
bloom to bloom to bloom,
not snapped by stubborn longing
into carnivorous sepals.

Throw out the devil of hoarding,
his bower-bird piracy
and magpie curios.
Let my green wants

be maple seeds
twirling into a ditch, my wishes
crackers flung over the transom
to battling gulls.

Goddess of discards,
let me be a waterfall
pouring a heedless mile,
stride barefoot over the drawbridge
to the plain road.

Elise Partridge, "Farewell Desires", Chameleon Hours: Poems, p. 32. Copyright © 2008 House of Anansi Press. Reproduced with permission.

This chapter presents a process for finding **themes**[1] in literary texts. It presumes that you have already carefully read, several times, the literary text you are analyzing. It also presumes that you are developing skills in analyzing texts, including an ability to work with important concepts that will help you to notice key evidence, such as symbols, **figurative language**, and **point of view**.

The concept of theme is critical in literary analysis essays, because theme is a central feature of literature that makes it worth reading and studying. In the discipline of English literature, we accept that literary texts express important ideas—not ideas that we must necessarily agree with, but ideas that would have consequences for us if they were true. We further accept that ideas themselves, as well as the ways in which literary texts create meaning, can be subtle and complicated. In the method presented by this book, the thesis statement, the main point of your essay, always identifies a theme. A statement of theme, in other words, is the thesis of your literary analysis essay. The body of your essay explains the complex way in which that theme is expressed.

Many writers have not yet finalized their thesis when they begin writing an essay. You should not feel that your statement of theme must be highly effective and in its final form before you begin. Instructors frequently find that the statements of theme that students write in their conclusions are more effective than the ones in their original theses. That is because students have gone through a process of discovery while writing their essays but have not taken advantage of their discoveries by rewriting their essays. When you develop a more sophisticated, insightful understanding of the literary text's theme, be prepared to go back and revise your essay accordingly.

One of the most exciting features of English literature for you as a student is that the process you are engaged in, writing a literary analysis essay, is fundamentally the same as the process in which your instructor is likely engaged. Many other disciplines are organized in such a way that it takes years before students become actively involved in doing what professionals in the discipline do. In English literature, however, students start in on that activity—analyzing literary texts—almost immediately. You will not be able to draw on the same experience, understanding, and skill as a professional literary critic,

---

[1]For brief definitions of bolded literary terms and some advice on how to use them in your analyses, see Appendix 5: Glossary of Literary Terms."

but that does not mean you will not be able to produce genuine, important insights into texts and their meaning. I know of no instructor in English literature who has not been struck at different times by the originality and importance of students' insights into the meaning of literary texts. Recognize that there are always new, significant things to be said about literary texts and that you have the potential to say them.

KEY POINTS

- The thesis of the literary analysis essay identifies a theme.
- Be prepared to revise your thesis as you write your essay.

\\ DEFINING THEME

A theme is an idea about the world, expressed by a literary text, of general importance to people.

This definition has three important components:

1. A theme is an idea about the world.

2. The idea is expressed by a literary text.

3. The idea expressed by the literary text is important to people in general, not just a small select group.

Consider the following statements:

1. The characters in the play who are loyal to their friends are happier in the end.

2. Loyalty to friends is more important than loyalty to ideas.

3. The theme of the play is that college students should support each other even if they support different political parties.

4. The play suggests that whether people value loyalty to friends or loyalty to ideas more, they must guard against the way that those with power exploit the concept of loyalty to preserve their privilege.

Statement 1 makes a potentially important claim, but it does not identify a theme. It expresses an idea about the play, rather than stating that the play expresses an idea about the world. **Descriptions of characters, no matter how insightful, are never statements of theme.**

Statement 2 expresses an important idea about the world, but it is not a theme because it does not state that the idea is expressed by a literary text. **A statement of theme must refer directly to a literary text.**

Statement 3 expresses an idea and asserts that the idea is expressed by a literary text. It does not, however, identify a theme. Even though it includes the word "theme," the idea it expresses does not apply to people in general; it only applies to college students. **A statement of theme cannot apply to only a specific group of people.**

It is frequently important to consider the significance of a literary text to a narrower group. It would be difficult, for example, to analyze *The Rez Sisters*, by Tomson Highway, effectively without considering that it has something important to say about conditions on First Nations reserves in Canada and the relations between men and women on those reserves. At some point, though, your analysis would need to move to a more general level. A poem written in 16th-century England, for example, may make an important comment about chivalric love, and your analysis of the poem would need to be aware of that focus of the poem. Your analysis will be more effective, however, if it also considers what the poem has to say about class values and human emotions more generally.

Statement 4 identifies a theme. It identifies an idea about the world; it states that the idea is expressed by a literary text and that the idea applies generally to people, not just to a narrow group.

The word "theme" is sometimes used inconsistently. Do not use "theme" to refer to the abstract topic of a text. It is incorrect, for instance, to say that the theme of a poem is love. The topic may be love. The theme in this case would be what the poem says about love, such as "love cannot exist without respect."

The history of the study of English literature is full of interesting controversies, and the term "theme" is sometimes connected to one of them. Some critics once approached literary texts assuming that they had one unique meaning and that every element in the text contributed to that meaning (that is, the literary work was "unified"). The literary text and its meaning—its theme—moreover, were taken to be independent of all but the most general of political and social forces.

Most contemporary literary critics now reject this view of literature and literary analysis, and some resist the word "theme" because they associate it with that rejected view. The term suggests for them the discredited idea that the text has only one meaning and that this meaning is always highly abstract and separate from concrete social concerns.

In this book, the term "theme" does not suggest such limitations. There are a number of alternatives to the word "theme," such as "an idea indirectly expressed by the text," "an argument that the text implies," or "an ideology the text endorses." If your instructor is not using this book, you should discover what terminology she or he prefers.

\\ DEBATING THEME

DEBATING WITH THE TEXT: AGREEING AND DISAGREEING WITH THEMES

You do not need to agree with the themes expressed by the texts they analyze. If you read enough, you will inevitably encounter texts that express themes with which you disagree. Literature is written, after all, by different people, living in different eras, influenced by different cultures, and with different personal experiences. Literary texts will inevitably express a wide range of ideas.

Sometimes students feel that they have to agree with the themes expressed by the works they study because they believe that their instructors agree with those themes. In fact, critics (including your instructors) frequently teach and analyze texts that express ideas with which they strongly disagree. (For example, a critic who is an atheist may analyze a text that implies that God exists, and a critic with religious beliefs may analyze a text that suggests that God does not exist.) You should not try to show that a text's theme is true or false, or even particularly relevant or important in a certain context (such as "today's society"). Critics' opinions of the ideas expressed by a text may be implicit in their analyses, but those opinions are not the point of the analyses.

Be prepared to study texts that express themes with which you disagree. Sometimes students feel that they should not have to read or analyze texts that express themes with which they strongly disagree or that they find offensive in some way. It is an important principle of the study of English literature that such objections are put aside. Studying a certain literary text does not mean having to accept it or agree with it, and we are obligated as critics to be willing to consider a broad range of literary texts.

DEBATING ABOUT TEXTS: AGREEING AND DISAGREEING ABOUT THEMES

Literary critics often disagree about what theme or themes a text expresses. Their discussions of these disagreements are an important part of what they do. This feature of literary studies leads some students to conclude that they can state anything they want about a literary text. The critic's task, however, is to make a convincing case that a text expresses a certain theme. It is no defence for a critic to say that an analysis is valid because "it is what I think." What a critic thinks must be supported by a convincing and well-proven argument in order to be taken seriously. This requirement applies equally to students writing essays for courses and to instructors writing essays for publication.

Some students worry about identifying the "correct" theme. Such students will sometimes persist in asking instructors what they think the theme of a text is, or they will do research to try to find confirmation that their analysis is correct. Rather than worrying about being correct, consider whether or not your analysis is convincing. Reasonable instructors will be open to a wide range of arguments about the theme of a particular text. An essay that makes a careful, convincing argument with which an instructor actually disagrees should be more successful than a sloppy or incomplete argument with which the instructor is in basic agreement.

KEY POINTS

- You are free to disagree with a theme expressed by a text you are analyzing.

- You are free to disagree with other critics about the theme of a text.

- You are not free to refuse to read or study texts that express themes with which you disagree.

\\ IDENTIFYING THEMES

Identifying theme is complicated, and students need to recognize that it takes considerable time and effort. Usually it is necessary to read a text at least a few times and to begin analyzing different features of it before beginning to form general conclusions about ideas the text expresses. As you gain experience, you will be able to consider more potential evidence in a text, ranging from the allegorical significance of characters in a novel to the importance of shifts in a poem's **metre**. The techniques described in this chapter should be applied along with close reading and rereading of texts. As you learn more about the features of different literary genres, you should apply your knowledge to your analyses. If, for example, your instructor has spent time discussing the idea of **imagery** and explaining how it functions in literary texts, you should be alert to imagery in the text that you are analyzing; look for opportunities to demonstrate your mastery of the concept by using the concept in your essay.

IDENTIFYING THEMES IN DRAMA AND PROSE FICTION

Drama and prose fiction are different from each other in many important ways. As critics, we need to pay attention to the features that are specific to each genre. Analyzing a play, for example, may require that we consider the importance of lighting and stage directions, while in a novel we might find that shifts in narrative point of view are important.

Usually, however, drama and prose fiction (and other genres such as film and poetry, when they tell a story) share a critical element for understanding theme, and that is **conflict**. The most useful technique for finding a theme in literary texts, especially drama and prose fiction, is to identify a main conflict, study the conflict to determine what it represents, and analyze the resolution of the conflict to determine what theme is expressed. The second and third of these steps, in particular, involve careful reading and detailed analysis. Consider the following simple story, a fable by Aesop:

THE GRASSHOPPER AND THE ANT

One summer's day a grasshopper was hopping about in a field, playing, singing, and having a good time. An ant passed by, carrying several stalks of wheat. The grasshopper said, "Why not come and play with me, instead of working so hard?"

"I need to work in order to store food for the winter," the ant replied. "You should be doing the same."

"Why bother about winter?" said the grasshopper. "There's lots of food right now." The ant ignored the grasshopper and simply went on its way, continuing to gather food.

When winter came, the grasshopper could find no food in the frozen fields. It slowly starved to death, while it watched the ants distributing the food they had worked hard all summer to collect and store.

Here is an outline of a simple analysis of the fable. (The simplicity of the story itself is deceptive; see "Identifying Complex Themes," later in the chapter.) It is not the only possible analysis, or even the best, but it presents a useful structure for finding theme in prose fiction and drama.

The conflict: The conflict is between the grasshopper and the ant. The grasshopper wants company in its play, while the ant has a conflicting desire: to continue working.

What the conflict represents: The grasshopper represents those who do not prepare for the future. The ants represent those who do prepare.

What is represented by the resolution of the conflict: The conflict's resolution presents negative consequences for the grasshopper and positive ones for the ants. In this way, the story suggests that the position represented by the ants is the preferred one, and thus it expresses its theme. The theme can be worded in many different ways, but most readers will agree that an important idea expressed by the fable is that one should work to prepare for the future, even when the work does not seem necessary at the moment.

The stories studied in English literature courses are almost always much more complicated than this fable, but the structure of the outline presented here can be followed successfully with complex texts. One of the most obvious elements that complicate prose fiction and drama is the ambiguity and difficulty frequently found in resolutions. The phrase "resolution of the conflict" does not imply that these literary texts will end in ways that establish winners and losers in the obvious manner of Aesop's fable. Finally, remember that identifying the conflict and what it represents is a process that involves multiple readings and the consideration of a variety of kinds of evidence, some of which is likely to be very subtle.

KEY POINTS

- When analyzing narrative texts, like drama and prose fiction, identify a main conflict.
- Establish what the conflict represents.
- Analyze what is represented by the resolution of the conflict.

IDENTIFYING THEMES IN POETRY

Many poems have conflicts similar to those found in fiction and drama; in interpreting such poems, the critic can apply techniques similar to those used for the other genres. Longer narrative poems, including epic poetry, have important and complicated conflicts. Even in a short poem, however, such as "Anecdote of the Jar," included along with the second essay in Appendix 2 (see page 95), we can identify a narrative and a conflict. The essay on that poem, "Unnatural Humanity: An Analysis of Wallace Stevens's 'Anecdote of the Jar,'" focuses on the conflict between the jar referred to in the title and the natural environment in which it is placed; then it looks at how that conflict is resolved. In many poems, however, such conflicts are not apparent. Whether or not there is an important conflict in a poem you are analyzing, poetry contrasts with other genres in the greater importance of formal elements that need to be analyzed. When you study a poem to determine its theme, remember to consider all of the features of its form as potential evidence.

When a poem does not "tell a story," or, in other words, does not have a narrative structure, it probably will not have an obvious conflict. The most important technique for finding the theme of such a poem is to identify the subject of the poem, consider that subject to determine what it represents, and analyze the poem to determine what attitude it expresses to the idea represented by its subject.

The poem's "subject" is what the poem is most obviously, concretely about. The subject can be a person, object, place, event, or other element. Sometimes, perhaps because of an anxiety about finding the "deeper meaning," students skip the step of identifying the subject and produce confusing and unconvincing analyses of a poem. If the speaker begins by describing a jar, it is important to notice that detail—that the subject of the poem is a jar—before going on to analysis.

The subject represents something beyond itself. Determining what the subject represents is a difficult task that almost always needs to be approached with caution. Resist the temptation to interpret every object or person in the poem as a **symbol**, with tenuous connections between the object or person and the more abstract idea it symbolizes. Such an approach leads to unconvincing analysis. Poetry does not mean whatever you want it to mean; your analysis must, as always, be convincing. It must be logical, thorough, and supported by details from the poem, and it must be clear to the reader of your essay why your interpretation is a valuable one.

The poem's "attitude" to its subject is equivalent to our own "attitudes" to things, meaning our feelings and thoughts about them. It is best to begin with very simple questions. Does the poem express a positive or negative attitude toward its subject? Is it admiring or critical? Such simple questions should then lead to more complicated ones, such as what is the specific quality that is being admired.

Theme in a Simple Poem

Consider the following short poem by Joyce Kilmer:

TREES

I think that I shall never see
A poem lovely as a tree.

A tree whose hungry mouth is prest
Against the earth's sweet flowing breast;

A tree that looks at God all day,
And lifts her leafy arms to pray;

A tree that may in summer wear
A nest of robins in her hair;

Upon whose bosom snow has lain;
Who intimately lives with rain.

Poems are made by fools like me,
But only God can make a tree.

From *Complete Poems*, published by Buccaneer.

Here is an outline of a simple analysis of the poem:

The subject: The subject of the poem is trees and poetry.

What the subject represents: The tree represents nature, which, the poem implies, is created by God, while poetry represents human creation.

The attitude of the poem: The attitude of the poem is that trees are better than poems. The theme is that our proper attitude toward nature should be humility and admiration, for nature is God's creation and surpasses anything that humans can create.

Theme in a Challenging Poem

Usually, the poems you will study in literature classes will be more challenging than Kilmer's "Trees." (The popularity of "Trees" probably has something to do with the directness with which it expresses a theme and its appeal to people who find poetry difficult and dissatisfying.) Consider the following poem by William Carlos Williams:

THE RED WHEELBARROW

so much depends
upon

a red wheel
barrow

glazed with rain
water

beside the white
chickens

By William Carlos Williams, from *THE COLLECTED POEMS: Volume I, 1909–1939*, copyright ©1938 by New Directions Publishing Corp. Reprinted by permission of New Directions Publishing Corp.

This poem, though short, is not as easy to analyze as "Trees" was. Here is an outline of a simple analysis of the poem:

The subject: The subject of the poem is a wheelbarrow.

What the subject represents: The wheelbarrow is a simple, human-made tool. A reasonable initial hypothesis is that the wheelbarrow represents simple, useful human creations.

The attitude of the poem: Williams's speaker says that "much depends" (1) on the wheelbarrow. In this way, the poem suggests that the wheelbarrow is important. The word "glazed" (5) often describes the surface finish of pottery (or, as one of my students once suggested, doughnuts), a finish that brings out the beauty of the work. This key word suggests that the wet wheelbarrow, enhanced by the rain, is beautiful. The poem, then, admires simple human creation both for its importance and its beauty. We're still near the starting point of our analysis, but we've made important progress, and you can probably see how that starting point could lead to the following conclusion: the theme of the poem is that human life is made meaningful by the beautiful combination of our labour and the natural world.

KEY POINTS

- Identify the subject of the poem.
- Establish what the subject of the poem represents.
- Analyze the poem's attitude to its subject.

Analyzing the Formal Features of Poetry

The chief way in which poetry is distinct from prose is that through its form poetry draws more attention to words as objects. Words refer to things, but they are also objects that have certain qualities, and their most obvious qualities are their sounds. The word "dog," for example, refers to a four-legged animal, among other things. The word also has a sound, which we are unlikely to think much about when we read it, unless the sound is called to our attention somehow. When we read "She has a hog, but he has a dog," the rhyme calls attention to the repeated sound of the vowel and the final consonant. The phrase "dogs do devilry" emphasizes the repeated sound of the initial consonant through **alliteration**. Rhyme and alliteration call our attention to the sounds of the words. They are examples of formal features of poetry.

In poetry, the effects of formal features combine with what the words mean. It is important that an analysis of a poem include a consideration of this combination, sometimes called "form and content" or "sound and sense." An analysis that does not consider the significance of a poem's formal features risks seeming incomplete. It can even give the impression that the critic has not noticed that the text being analyzed is a poem.

The formal features of a poem can be identified without knowing what the words mean. For example, you only need to know how words are pronounced, not what they mean, to tell whether they rhyme; rhyme, therefore, is a formal feature of poetry. In contrast, you do need to know what the words mean in order to tell whether a description contains **figurative language**. Figurative language, therefore, is *not* a formal feature of poetry.

Many of the devices that direct our attention to "form"—to the qualities of words as objects—have names. The terms in the glossary (see Appendix 5) that refer to formal features of poetry are as follows: alliteration, **assonance**, **blank verse**, caesura, **consonance, couplet, enjambment, fixed forms, free verse, heroic couplet**, metre, **onomatopoeia**, rhyme, **sonnet, stanza**, and **verse paragraph**. The definitions include tips for analyzing these formal features.

Formal features of a poem can be identified without knowing what the words mean. For example, you only need to know how words are pronounced, not what they mean, to tell whether they rhyme; rhyme, therefore, is a formal feature of poetry. In contrast, you do need to know what the words mean in order to tell whether a description is a metaphor. Metaphors, therefore, are not formal features of poetry.

Focus your attention on a poem's formal features only after you have analyzed its content carefully. With very few exceptions, formal features do not generate meaning on their own. They emphasize what is conveyed by the poem's content. In Thomas Wyatt's sonnet "Whoso List to Hunt," for example, the speaker describes his chase after a deer: "but as she fleeth afore, / Fainting I follow" (6–7). The alliteration emphasizes the speaker's breathlessness as he runs after the deer, but it will do so only after the line has been understood to describe the speaker continuing his pursuit despite his fatigue.

Assonance, consonance, and rhyme can emphasize words and suggest connections between them. Read the poem out loud. Note whether the words that are connected through their similar sounds are also connected by the poem's meaning. If the poem somehow suggests that one thing or idea has something to do with another, and these things or ideas are identified with words that rhyme, the rhyme may emphasize the connection. If the sense of the poem suggests that certain words are important, it is worth noting if assonance, consonance, or rhyme also draws our attention to the words, thus emphasizing that importance. (The essay in Appendix 2 entitled "Unnatural Humanity: An Analysis of Wallace Stevens's 'Anecdote of the Jar'" has an example of such an analysis of rhyme; see page 96.)

Assonance, consonance, rhyme, and alliteration can create an onomatopoeic effect. The line from Wyatt's sonnet quoted previously is an example of the way this feature can work. None of the words in the line is onomatopoeic on its own, but in a series they create a sound that some critics associate with the action they describe: the speaker's struggle for breath as he pursues the deer.

When studying the formal features of the poem, consider the overall effect of a regular pattern of rhyme—a rhyme scheme. If you observe that there is such a scheme, or even if you think there might be one, marking the rhyme can help you to notice the pattern in detail and make it easier to comment on it (see "rhyme" in the glossary in Appendix 5 for instructions on marking rhyme schemes). Rhyme schemes frequently create a sense of unity. Sets of rhymes can create an impression of sections in a poem, even if no spaces mark a separation between one part of a poem and another. If the rhyme scheme creates the impression of different sections, consider whether the shift from one section to another emphasizes a shift from one idea to another, or perhaps a shift in **tone**.

Consider whether changes in metre are related to changes in content. To analyze metre, read the poem out loud. If you think the poem may have a regular metre, read a few lines carefully, out loud, and scan them. Your scansion will help you to perceive the metre and make it easier to refer to it in your analysis. (See "metre" in Appendix 5 for an explanation of "scan" and "scansion.")

A shift in metre often reinforces the meaning of the words. A shift from iambic to spondaic, for example, can contribute to a shift to a more insistent, even angry tone, or it can simply emphasize the words in the spondaic feet. A pause in a line—a caesura—can suggest a hesitation on the part of the speaker, or it can call attention to the relationship between what is said before and what is said after, in a single line. The meaning of the caesura, like that of other formal features, is related to the content of the line.

Your consideration of the formal features of the poem will include studying the relationship between verse form and meaning. Certain verse forms and fixed forms are associated in English literature with certain subjects and tones. Limericks, for instance, are funny. Sonnets were originally serious poems about unrequited love, but their range was extended to serious spiritual matters and then to serious topics more generally. The expectation that a fixed form poem will deal with certain topics in certain ways becomes part of the poem's meaning. When analyzing a poem, observe whether it is an example of a fixed form that you have covered in the course. Consider making a concise comment on the form's significance in relation to the poem's content.

Whether or not a poem is an example of a fixed form, observe the arrangement of words on the page. Note whether the lines are of a regular length, whether there are spaces between sections of the poem, and whether there are any striking features of the poem's appearance that draw attention, such as lines of one word. Note whether spaces between stanzas or verse paragraphs emphasize changes in topic, shifts in tone, and so on. (The way in which such sections frequently work to emphasize changes in content is like the way in which indenting at the beginning of paragraphs, a formal feature of prose, emphasizes a change. In your own essays, this formal feature makes it easier for the reader to understand your meaning by signalling a change from one idea to another.)

When analyzing poems written in free verse, take note of unusual shapes or patterns of shapes formed by the words on the page, and consider whether they have any relationship to content. Some critics, for example, have noted that the short verse paragraphs of "The Red Wheelbarrow" are similar in shape to a wheelbarrow, and that this similarity emphasizes the poem's assertion of the importance of the wheelbarrow and what it represents.

Speculating too fancifully about the implications of a poem's shape can detract from your entire analysis, so be cautious. Usually, the poem's appearance will not have as direct a relationship to content as in the example of the wheelbarrow. Consider, instead, how the appearance of the poem might draw attention to certain phrases or words by isolating them on the page. The poem might draw attention to a lack of unity by separating phrases that would otherwise belong together in a phrase or sentence. Think about how the arrangement of the words and lines suggests how the poem should sound when read aloud, and how that sound might be connected to content.

KEY POINTS

- Analyses of poems should consider their formal features.
- Do not analyze formal features until you have some understanding of the poem's content.
- Consider the ways in which formal features emphasize words or phrases, and create connections between words and phrases.
- Consider the significance of the poem's overall form, whether it is an example of a fixed form or free verse.

IDENTIFYING COMPLEX THEMES

Literary texts may have more than one theme, and the themes may even be contradictory. This thematic complexity can be found even in very simple stories. In addition to the obvious theme of "The Grasshopper and the Ant," we could consider what the fable suggests about the duty society has to those of its members who lack the wisdom to care for themselves adequately. The ants do not come to the dying grasshopper's assistance at the end of the story, so we could argue that the fable suggests that those who have the foresight to take care of themselves owe nothing at all to those who lack that foresight.

Remember that you are not expected to agree or disagree with the theme that you identify. Many readers will agree that it is wise to prepare for the future, and many will disagree with the idea that people who are unwise or self-destructive have lost all claim to our support, but as literary critics we do not let that agreement or disagreement affect our judgment as to what theme is expressed.

As with the fable, the simplicity of a poem such as "Trees" can be deceptive, and a close examination may reveal other themes. Consider, for instance, the way in which the description of the tree relies on various tropes (figures of speech), most notably personification. The tree's value seems to depend on the speaker's attaching human qualities to it. Perhaps another theme of the poem is that although the human imagination may seem inferior to nature, nature and God are valuable to us only when we can see them as reflections of our own personalities.

The texts studied in English literature classes are almost always much more complicated than Aesop's fables and Kilmer's "Trees." Be very cautious about reducing a complicated text to a simple idea. Everything in the literary text is potential evidence that develops its conflict or its attitude, and, therefore, the range of ideas represented. Your instructor is likely to discuss with you the characters, setting, structure, possible symbols, images, **allusions**, rhyme, metre, and many other elements of literature that contribute to our understanding of what a single work means. Be prepared to read and reread very carefully, building your own understanding of what issues a work raises.

\\ A CHECKLIST FOR EFFECTIVE STATEMENTS OF THEME

Remember that effective statements do not need to identify ideas that you think are true; rather, they need to identify ideas that meet the criteria of a theme and are supported by evidence from the literary text. When developing an understanding of a text's theme, write down your preliminary thoughts. Experiment with different ideas about what the conflict represents and what is represented by the resolution of the conflict. Make notes about the ideas that come to you when the text is being discussed in class. Use the following checklist to review your statement of theme and improve its effectiveness after you have spent considerable time analyzing the text. The more straightforward guidelines on the checklist are at the beginning, the more difficult and abstract ones at the end. For most students, developing confidence and expertise in creating effective statements of theme with respect to these final points takes considerable practice.

1. Connect the idea to the text rather than making it seem like an independent idea that you are trying to show to be true.

   Ineffective: The ways people think about themselves are limited by the language they are able to use.

   This sentence does not connect the idea to a literary work, so it does not actually identify a theme.

> *Effective:* The novel suggests that people should recognize that the ways they think about themselves are controlled by the forces that control language.

2. Identify a complete idea, not just a topic.

> *Ineffective:* The theme of the play is about love.

The sentence only identifies a topic, so it is not a theme. It needs to specify what the play states about love. Part of the problem is the use of the word "about." If you substitute the word "that" for "about," it should lead to a more complete statement identifying an idea.

> *Effective:* A central theme of the play is that the tendency of modern cultures to present certain understandings of love as "natural" is destructive.

3. Identify an idea that applies to people in general, not just to the literary text and not just to a specific group of people with narrow interests.

> *Ineffective:* An important theme of the story is that Bob's emotional problems are caused by his own selfishness.

The sentence is a description of a character in the story, so it does not identify an idea that the text expresses about the world.

> *Effective:* An important theme of the story is that individual selfishness is always connected to the social systems in which people are embedded.

> *Ineffective:* One of the play's main themes is that people who live near swimming pools should warn their children about using the pools without permission.

The sentence identifies an idea that is of interest only to a narrow group of people, so it is not a theme.

> *Effective:* One of the play's main themes is that we cannot care for the most vulnerable among us without recognizing the vulnerability within ourselves.

4. Identify an important idea. The idea must not be true by definition or so weakly expressed that one cannot reasonably disagree with it.

> *Ineffective:* The novel implicitly argues that it is bad to be cruel.

Being "cruel" is "bad" by definition, so we have not learned anything from the statement. It is an ineffective statement of theme.

> *Effective:* The novel implicitly argues that cruelty needs to be understood as an expression of power imbalances in a culture, not simply as the responsibility of bad individuals.

Ineffective: One theme of the novel is that sometimes terrible experiences can hurt people very badly.

The idea identified is so obviously true that no one could reasonably disagree with it. Note that if on one occasion, in the history of the world, someone was hurt by a bad experience, then the statement is true. Avoid words such as "sometimes" and "can" in thesis statements, as they frequently lead to this kind of weakness.

Effective: One theme of the novel is that the wisest choice people have when dealing with trauma is to work to recognize and accept the ways it changes their fundamental identities.

5. Do not reduce the idea the text expresses to a simple "moral."

Ineffective: The story expresses the idea that what goes around comes around.

The statement is ineffective because it suggests that the story is equivalent to a cliché. (This example is a specific version of point 8, "emptying the plot.")

Effective: The story expresses the idea that eventually the contradictions within capitalism are destructive even for those who seem to benefit from its divisions of wealth.

6. Do not present the text as being neutral toward something, as though it seeks only to point out that something exists. Make it clear that the work expresses an attitude to its topic or identifies an important consequence that is connected to it.

Ineffective: The poem implies that there is no God.

The statement is ineffective because it does not show why the idea is important. The idea that God does not exist is certainly important, but what is the attitude of the poem to that idea, or what consequences does the poem suggest follow from that idea?

Effective: The poem implies that there is no God, so our only choice is to resign ourselves to lives without meaning.

Effective: The poem celebrates the absence of God and insists that people can create meaning through their relations with others.

7. Do not "pluralize the plot." In other words, do not construct an idea simply by taking characters and elements of the plot to represent many examples of what they are.

Ineffective: One theme of the story is that superheroes always defeat supervillains.

The statement is ineffective because it only summarizes, in the plural, a key element of the plot: the superhero defeats the supervillain.

Less ineffective: One theme of the story is that good always triumphs over evil.

8. Do not "empty the plot." In other words, do not give the impression that much of the detail of the text is unimportant.

Ineffective: An important theme of the play is that good always triumphs over evil.

The statement is ineffective because most works of literature are more complicated than the statement suggests and imply more specific ideas about the nature of good and evil.

Effective: The theme of the play is that the evil that threatens society always comes from outside, and that in order to combat it we must rely on forces that are independent of and unchecked by all our social institutions.

Remember that literary works may express many themes and that these themes may even be contradictory. Identifying a theme does not mean that you are asserting that it is the only theme, and it does not mean that you agree with the idea that the text expresses.

EXERCISE SET 3.1—IDENTIFYING STATEMENTS OF THEME

In Exercises 3.1 A and 3.1 B, some of the sentences identify a theme. Some do not identify a theme, either because

a) they do not identify an idea about the world, or

b) the idea they identify does not express an important truth of general importance to people, or

c) they do not connect the idea they identify to a literary text.

Indicate whether each sentence identifies a theme, and, if it does not, indicate whether it is because of reason a, b, or c. Remember that you can identify a theme without using the word "theme."

Exercise 3.1 A (Answers are in Appendix 4)

1. God does not exist.

2. The main character is a bad person.

3. One theme of the story is that the main character is a bad person.

4. The novel suggests that the main character is a bad person.

5. An important theme of the play is that Vancouverites should be careful about water consumption.

6. The poem implicitly argues that we have a greater duty to our friends than to our country.

7. A central theme of the story is that what may seem to be "natural" ideas of friendship are socially constructed and serve those with power.

8. Love is nothing more than a destructive illusion.

9. The play suggests that the main character is not evil, but rather is the victim of her evil culture.

10. An important theme of the poem is that individual freedom is dangerously fragile.

Exercise 3.1 B

1. One theme of the story is that college students should study hard.

2. Without acknowledging our relationships, it is impossible for us to have meaningful lives.

3. The novel argues that society is not responsible for the failures of the characters.

4. A theme of the poem is that it is dangerous to fail to recognize that people are fundamentally bad.

5. The story expresses the idea that common distinctions between emotion and reason serve destructive beliefs about gender.

6. One theme of the play is about class conflict.

7. A main theme of the novel is that love is more important than money; the main character's desire for money is a product of his impoverished upbringing.

8. The story dramatizes the notion that it is a terrible mistake to believe that we are capable of genuine self-understanding.

9. One main theme of the story is that Canada in the 1950s was a country gripped by fear.

10. Implicitly, the play makes the case that the idea of "honour" is actually a tool used to marginalize those who reject social norms.

11. An important theme of the novel is that the narrator's husband is a complex private symbol of the destructiveness of male domination.

12. A central theme of the story is that the yellow wallpaper represents the conventions of society that trap and subdue women.

Exercise 3.1 C

1. Identify a theme in the literary text that you worked with in Exercise 2.4 C, questions 1 and 2.

2. Using the checklist for effective statements of theme, review the theme you identified. Choose a point in the Checklist for Effective Statements of Theme that you think identifies a feature of your statement that needs improvement, and revise your statement of theme.

When you have a provisional thesis for your essay, you are probably ready to begin shaping your ideas and observations into an argument, the essay's final form. The argument proves your thesis. Remember that the writing process involves rereading, revising your ideas, and developing your insights further as you go along. The thesis is part of this process; it can and probably should be changed as your essay develops.

\\ THE DIFFERENCE BETWEEN A LOGICAL SEQUENCE AND A LIST

An argument moves through a sequence of logically connected steps leading to a conclusion. If your argument is clear, convincing, and logically structured, your reader will agree with each main point you make, and the entire sequence of main points will prove your thesis.

Do not confuse a logical sequence with a list. Many students are accustomed to writing essays that have the structure of a list. Each paragraph in list essays presents one reason that the thesis is true. In fact, theses for such essays frequently refer to these reasons by number, in statements such as "There were three main causes of World War One." A list of this type is not the same as an argument, which proceeds by logical steps. Some instructors may still ask that students use a list structure; but at the college and university level, most prefer that the essay make a coherent, logically sequential argument, building toward proving a thesis.

A sign of the difference between a list structure and a logically sequential structure is the order in which points are made. Students writing list essays often wonder which point to begin with, sometimes asking whether it should be the most important or the least important. There is no *logical* reason to begin with any one point in a list essay because one point does not depend on what has been established in the previous point. In contrast, in an essay that has a logically sequential structure, the point with which you need to begin is connected to your thesis, and the following points progress, each depending on the one before. Ask yourself this question, when beginning an essay with a sequential structure: What is the first thing that I need to prove?

Repeat key terms from your thesis in your claims. This repetition will help make your argument clear and coherent. The key terms will act as a guide to the reader, who needs to keep track of the relationship between each step of the argument and the thesis. Such repetition becomes more important as your essays grow longer and more complex. (Five paragraphs is a common minimum for essays, but it is certainly not the maximum.) A common weakness in literary analysis essays, at all levels, is a lack of clarity. Writers know what they mean and think, so they tend to overestimate how clear they are being. *Key-word repetition* is a very important tool in overcoming this problem.

Note that if your claims are connected to your thesis and logically ordered, they will create a sense of transition from one paragraph to the next. The transition is accomplished by the completion of a discussion of one claim, with its key terms connected to the thesis, and a logically connected new claim, which introduces the new key term or terms that logically follow.

Your final claim should be similar to your thesis. The final analytical paragraph must show that the literary text expresses the theme you identified. If you have succeeded in developing a logically structured essay, the reader will be prepared for your final claim and have a sense that the argument is now complete.

KEY POINTS

- A literary analysis essay has the structure of an argument.
- An argument is a sequence of logically related steps, not a list.
- Connect your claims to your thesis by repeating key terms.
- In order to complete your argument, the wording of your final claim should be close to the wording of your thesis.

SAMPLE OUTLINES
Sample Outline: List Structure

Thesis: Through the narrator's writing, her resistance to her husband, and her efforts to rescue the woman in the wallpaper, the story suggests that the imagination is irrepressible.

Claim 1:   The narrator's persistence in writing suggests that the imagination is irrepressible.

Claim 2:   The narrator's resistance to her husband implies that the imagination is irrepressible.

Claim 3:   The narrator's efforts to rescue the woman in the wallpaper suggest that the imagination is irrepressible.

Conclusion

Note how each claim makes one of the points made in the thesis. The claims appear in the same order in which they appear in the thesis.

Sample Outline: Logical Sequence Structure

The logical sequence that a literary analysis essay follows leads up to a claim that, like the thesis (and in very similar, if not identical, terms), identifies a theme.

Thesis: "The Yellow Wallpaper" suggests that the imagination is irrepressible and that any attempt to stifle it is deeply destructive.

Claim 1:   The story's narrator represents human imagination.

Claim 2:   The narrator's husband's treatment of her represents an attempt to stifle imagination.

Claim 3:   The narrator's response to her treatment reveals the irrepressibility of the imagination.

Claim 4:   The condition of the narrator and her husband at the story's resolution suggests that attempts to stifle imagination are deeply destructive.

Conclusion

Note how the first claim does not say anything about the strength of the imagination, attempts to stifle the imagination, or the destructiveness of attempts to stifle the imagination. **The argument begins by establishing a small part of what needs proving**: the story involves imagination in some way. Only once it is established that the narrator represents imagination does her husband's treatment of her become relevant to a discussion of human imagination. Students frequently feel that they must begin by proving almost the entire thesis. Instead, take only a small first step. Prove the first thing that needs proving.

If you carefully review each claim, you will see that each one repeats more key words from the thesis. This increase in the number of key words is a common feature of the argument structure. The argument is building toward proving the entire thesis, and so it is including more of the important concepts as it moves along. The repetition of key terms also helps the reader to keep the entire argument in mind and to understand the connection between each stage of the argument and the thesis.

The final claim mentions the resolution of the conflict. In literary texts in which plot is important—such as most plays, stories, and novels—the resolution of the conflict must be included in the final claim. Your argument should not simply follow the order of the events in the plot (doing so is a dangerous sign that the essay is simply plot summary), but the resolution must be analyzed last because of its importance in the expression of theme. When analyzing literary texts in which plot is of considerably less importance—such as most poems—the final claim must deal with the attitude of the text to what is represented by its subject.

KEY POINTS

- Do not try to prove the entire thesis with your first claim.
- The number of key terms from the thesis usually increases with each claim.

EXERCISE SET 4.1—UNDERSTANDING ARGUMENT STRUCTURE

Exercise 4.1 A (Answers are in Appendix 4)

1. Read the claims in the list structure outline in the following order: 3, 2, 1. Does the argument still make sense?

2. Read the claims in the logical sequence structure outline in the following order: 4, 2, 1, 3. Does the argument still make sense?

3. Identify the key words in the thesis of the logical sequence structure outline.

4. Identify the key words in the claims that repeat the key words in the thesis. (The words may be in slightly different form.)

5. Identify the key words in the following thesis (the words that should be repeated in the essay's claims):

   One of the main themes of the poem is that people must resist their dangerous tendency to see themselves as separate from nature.

Exercise 4.1 B

1. Identify the key words in the following thesis (the words that should be repeated in the essay's claims):

   > The play implicitly argues that our world is absurd and that no individual response to absurdity can rescue us from desperation and violence.

2. Which key term from the thesis above is most likely to be included in the first claim?

3. Identify the problem in the following claim, which is the final claim of the essay:

   > The resolution of the conflict suggests that the main character no longer believes that any response he has to absurdity can rescue him from desperation and violence.

Exercise 4.1 C

1. Identify the key words in the statement of theme you developed in Exercise 3.1 C, question 1.

2. Write a series of analytical claims that form a logical argument in support of the statement of theme you developed in Exercise 3.1 C, question 1.

3. Underline the words in your claims that repeat the key words in your thesis. (Each claim should repeat at least one key term from the thesis.)

\\ ORGANIZATIONAL PARAGRAPHS AND THE TITLE

The argument of a literary analysis essay is made up of analytical paragraphs. In order for the argument to be clear, the essay includes several other components that help the reader to follow the argument; the organizational paragraphs—the introductory paragraph, the concluding paragraph, the transitional paragraphs—and the title all help organize the essay in the reader's mind, making the argument easier to follow and more likely to be convincing.

The title and organizational paragraphs are useful for the writing process as they help writers to keep their arguments clear. Do not feel, however, that you need to have your introductory paragraph in its final form before beginning the rest of your essay. The introductory paragraph and other organizational paragraphs are usually the last to be revised for the final draft. You may find, for example, that as your essay develops you are analyzing evidence you had not originally planned to consider. It is not difficult to go back to your introduction and adjust it to be consistent with the new direction your analysis has taken.

INTRODUCTORY PARAGRAPHS
Introductory Paragraphs and Their Four Components

Common advice for writers of introductory paragraphs is to begin with a general statement and move to a more specific statement, the thesis. This advice applies to introductions to literary analysis essays. The paragraph should begin by making a general statement and then move toward the specific point about the literary text that the essay will make. **The introduction does not begin the argument; it simply says what the argument will be.** The introduction should be brief, in part because the essays you write in first- and second-year English courses tend to be short, in many cases with specific word limitations. You need to present the essentials only, so you can develop your analysis as much as possible. The four essentials are the following:

1. **Opening—author, text, and abstract topic:** Students sometimes have difficulty determining how general their opening should be and how to make that opening interesting. Instructors sometimes read essays that begin with statements such as "Since the beginning of time, people have always…." Such statements are an attempt to begin generally and to capture the reader's interest, but they are too vague. They require that the introduction make too big a leap to the specific thesis. The appropriate place to begin has to do with the interests of the audience, which cares about the literary text you are analyzing and the meaning of that text. **The opening should identify the text, its author, and one, or perhaps two, of its abstract topics, such as love, death, maturity, or racism.** The list of potential abstract topics is endless. Such an opening will establish for readers that your essay will indeed focus on the literary text that they are interested in, and that it will address the issue of the text's meaning. It will also signal to your instructor that you understand a fundamental principle of literary analysis: literary texts express ideas.

2. **Evidence preview:** The next step in the introductory paragraph is to narrow the topic by identifying what evidence from the text the essay will focus on. Note that you do not present the evidence in detail. Introductions rarely include quotations. **Simply state, briefly and without quoting, what evidence the essay will analyze.** The evidence could be one or more key scenes in a novel, one character in a play, a pattern of imagery in a poem, or a combination of different kinds of evidence.

3. **Links between the evidence and the thesis statement:** The introduction needs to state that there is a connection between the evidence the essay will focus on and the theme that will be identified in the thesis. In the simplest version of this step, all you need to do is assert that such a connection exists. State that the evidence is important to the theme of the text. In a more thorough introduction, you can state something brief about the nature of the connection. State what is important about the evidence that connects it to the theme. The link can be included in the sentence that previews the evidence.

4. **Thesis statement:** The final sentence in the introductory paragraph is the thesis. The thesis identifies a theme (which must be consistent with the abstract topic). Sometimes students find the distinction between "theme" and "thesis" confusing. The theme is the idea expressed by the literary text. The thesis is your idea that the literary text expresses a certain theme. If you find the distinction difficult, try thinking of the literary text as being like a person. You are asked to write an essay explaining what the person thinks about college education. Your thesis might go like this:

> Anna thinks that college education is the solution to all of the problems of the human race.

Your thesis is not the same thing as what Anna thinks. You do not necessarily think that a college education is the solution to all of the problems of the human race. You think that Anna thinks so. Similarly, your thesis in an essay analyzing a literary text tells us what the story or poem "thinks," but it is not the same as that theme.

Working With Introductory Paragraphs

Sample introduction (a simple version):

> One of the topics of Alex B. Rankin's novel *Brilliantine* is love. Several key images in the novel are important to one of its main themes. This main theme is that the idea of true love is a destructive illusion.

Sample introduction (an ambitious version):

> Alex B. Rankin's ironic novel *Brilliantine* is a complex examination of the cultural significance of love. A subtle pattern of imagery in the novel develops an impression of the romantic and yet selfish world view of Jill, the narrator. The connection between this imagery and Jill's world view is key to the novel's theme: although love is at the centre of modern culture, the way in which it is connected to premodern ideas of class and privilege makes it a destructive cultural force.

Note that in each of the sample introductory paragraphs, the essay's argument does not yet begin. The introductory paragraph does not start to analyze the novel. It introduces the analysis.

One of the distinctions between the simple version and the more ambitious version is that the ambitious one, in its opening sentence, asserts that the topic of the essay, in this case a novel, is complicated. It is useful, not only in English literature but in other disciplines as well, to signal to the reader that you recognize that the topic you are writing on is complicated. If you suggest that the topic is simple, your instructor—whether in history, philosophy, or sociology—is likely to disagree. Simply asserting in your introduction that the topic is complicated does not, of course, accomplish a great deal. Your argument will need to respond to the complexity of the topic.

Each of the essays in Appendix 2 has an introduction that follows the structure outlined here. You can read those introductory paragraphs and note the key components in each to reinforce your understanding of how introductions work.

EXERCISE SET 4.2—UNDERSTANDING INTRODUCTORY PARAGRAPHS

Exercise 4.2 A (Answers are in Appendix 4)

1. In the first sample introductory paragraph, identify each of the four components described at the beginning of this chapter.
2. In the first sample introductory paragraph, identify the key words in the first sentence.
3. In the first sample introductory paragraph, identify the words in the thesis statement that repeat key words in the first sentence (the words may be in slightly different form).

Exercise 4.2 B

1. In the second sample introductory paragraph, identify each of the four components described at the beginning of this chapter.
2. In the second sample introductory paragraph, identify the key words in the first sentence.
3. In the second sample introductory paragraph, identify the words in the thesis statement that repeat key words in the first sentence (the words may be in slightly different form).

Exercise 4.2 C

1. Write an introductory paragraph that concludes with the statement of theme you developed in your answer to Exercise 3.1 C, question 2.
2. Identify each of the four key components in your introductory paragraph.
3. Identify the key words in the first sentence of your introductory paragraph.
4. Identify the words in your thesis statement that repeat key words from the first sentence (the words may be in slightly different form).

TRANSITIONAL PARAGRAPHS

Transitional Paragraphs and Their Two Components

An essay will be more effective if readers can keep its thesis and the overall argument in their minds as they proceed. Key-word repetition is one of the ways to help readers follow the argument and be aware of the relationship between what they are reading and the thesis. In longer essays (most commonly written in third year and after), another important tool for helping readers to follow the argument is the transitional paragraph. Such paragraphs do not contain analysis; rather, they alert readers to the shift from one section of an argument to the next. If your essay is long enough that it has several sections of several paragraphs, consider including transitional paragraphs between the sections. The transitional paragraph should be brief, and it should contain the following two components:

1. **Review:** The transitional paragraph begins with a brief review of what has been established or accomplished in the section just concluded. This review encourages readers to think of the connection between the preceding paragraphs and the thesis. It helps readers to keep their place in a complicated argument.

2. **Preview:** The preview looks at the next section of the argument. Sometimes writers will simply state what they will discuss next. It is more effective to state why the essay will move on to this topic. The reason should have to do with the logic of the argument.

Working With Transitional Paragraphs

Sample transitional paragraph (a simple version):

> It is clear, then, that the characters believe that they feel love. It is also evident that in the world of the novel, their love is considered "true." It is now necessary to show that the novel suggests that this love is an illusion, in a way that implies that true love is always illusory.

Sample transitional paragraph (a more ambitious version):

> Thus, the tropes with which Jill persistently describes herself and others reveal both the value she attaches to spontaneity and her confidence that a profound truth, one that is challenging to convention and liberating of the self, is available through a serious contemplation of nature. These values are clearly romantic. In order to show how these romantic values are connected to love and love's position in modern culture, the way in which they are linked to selfishness needs to be established.

EXERCISE SET 4.3—UNDERSTANDING TRANSITIONAL PARAGRAPHS

Exercise 4.3 A (Answers are in Appendix 4)

1. Identify the two key components in the first sample transitional paragraph.

2. Identify the key words in the first sample transitional paragraph that repeat key words from the thesis of the first sample introductory paragraph in the preceding section (see page 49).

Exercise 4.3 B

1. Identify the two key components in the second sample transitional paragraph.

2. Identify the key words in the second sample transitional paragraph that repeat key words from the thesis of the second sample introductory paragraph in the preceding section (see page 49).

Exercise 4.3 C

1. Write a paragraph that makes a transition from one claim to the next in the sequence of claims you wrote for Exercise 4.1 C, question 2.

2. Identify the words in your transitional paragraph that repeat key words from the thesis you wrote for Exercise 3.1 C, question 1.

CONCLUDING PARAGRAPHS
Concluding Paragraphs and Their Three Components

The final analytical paragraph in body of your essay completes your argument, so in an important sense the concluding paragraph comes after the essay is finished. Little more needs to be said, so conclusions should be brief. The concluding paragraph should reinforce the readers' understanding of the entire argument of your essay, and it should provoke readers to think further about the text you have been analyzing. The conclusion signals that you and your readers are engaged in a shared project of understanding your specific text and literature in general. The conclusion has more flexibility than the other paragraphs in the essay, but no new evidence is introduced and no new analysis is presented. Keep your audience in mind; avoid going off topic by discussing how much you do or do not like the text, how important it is for your life, and so on. Here are three components that may be included in an effective conclusion:

1. **The Summary:** The summary briefly restates the essay's thesis. It does not simply repeat the thesis word for word, but rather presents it again, taking advantage of the understanding developed by the essay. One way to present the thesis again without simply repeating it is to refer to its broader implications. If you have argued that a text suggests something about religion, for example, your summary might make a connection between this topic and the broader one of spirituality. In longer essays, expand your summary to include a review of the important steps in your argument.

2. **The Acknowledgment of Limitation:** Your essay will not have considered all of the implications of the text you analyze, or all of the evidence. An effective conclusion may include an acknowledgment of the limitations of your analysis.

3. **The New Possibility:** The acknowledgement of limitation can lead easily into this component, in which you suggest a topic, or issue, or focus of analysis that your essay has not covered but which it might raise in the minds of your readers.

Working With Concluding Paragraphs

Sample concluding paragraph (a simple version):

> True love is never really true, *Brilliantine* asks us to believe. The novel suggests that if we think this illusion is real, our lives will suffer for it. By questioning love, the novel questions all of our most important values and asks whether our unthinking acceptance of them is dangerous. Much more than the novel's imagery could be analyzed to investigate this idea, as well as other topics this essay has not considered, such as the novel's attitude to the tension between the individual and the community.

Sample concluding paragraph (a more ambitious version):

> *Brilliantine* criticizes love for its insidious and anachronistic importing of traditional, class-bound conceptions of the self into the modern world. The imagery throughout the novel that suggests this covert feature of our concept of love is subtle, implying that the destructive effects of love are similarly difficult to identify and respond to. The novel thus invites us to consider how all of our important values are connected to complicated histories in ways we need to struggle to understand. A further study might consider how, for example, the novel's treatment of the idea of freedom is tied to a complicated history of ideas about liberty.

Each of the essays in Appendix 2 has a conclusion that follows the structure outlined here. You can read those concluding paragraphs and note the key components in each to reinforce your understanding of how conclusions work.

EXERCISE SET 4.4—UNDERSTANDING CONCLUDING PARAGRAPHS

Exercise 4.4 A (Answers are in Appendix 4)

1. Identify the three key components in the first sample concluding paragraph.
2. Identify the key words in the first sample concluding paragraph that are repeated from the thesis of the first sample introductory paragraph (see page 49).

Exercise 4.4 B

1. Identify the three key components in the second sample concluding paragraph.
2. Underline the key words in the second sample concluding paragraph that are repeated from the thesis of the second sample introductory paragraph (see page 49).

Exercise 4.4 C

1. Write a concluding paragraph for the essay outlined in your answer to Exercise 4.1 C, question 2.

2. Identify the key components of your concluding paragraph.

TITLES

Titles and Their Three Components

A good title is informative. A good title can also be clever, odd, and even puzzling, but these more imaginative elements should not mean that the title does not give a clear idea of an essay's subject. Someone doing research on a topic related to your essay should be able to understand from your title whether or not your essay might be useful.

The title of a literary analysis essay should identify three things:

1. The text being discussed in the essay

2. The author of the text

3. The focus of the essay

Two Styles of Titles

STYLE 1   Style 1 identifies a topic with a noun or list of nouns and connects it to the author and the work with the word "in."

  Example: Identity in Shaena Lambert's *Radiance*

  Example: Identity and Culture in Shaena Lambert's *Radiance*

STYLE 2   Style 2 identifies a topic with a phrase that comes before a colon.

  Example: Struggling with Identity: An Analysis of Shaena Lambert's *Radiance*

  Example: The Culture of Identity: An Analysis of Shaena Lambert's *Radiance*

COMBINED STYLE   The two styles can be combined to produce a more ambitious title.

  Example: Culture and Class: An Analysis of Identity Formation in Shaena Lambert's *Radiance*

EXERCISE SET 4.5—UNDERSTANDING TITLES

Exercise 4.5 A (Answers are in Appendix 4)

1. Create a title in Style 1 for an essay beginning with the first sample introductory paragraph (see page 49).

2. Create a title in Style 2 for an essay beginning with the first sample introductory paragraph.

3. Create a title that combines Style 1 and Style 2 for an essay beginning with the first sample introductory paragraph.

Exercise 4.5 B

1. Create a title in Style 1 for an essay beginning with the second sample introductory paragraph (see page 49).

2. Create a title in Style 2 for an essay beginning with the second sample introductory paragraph.

3. Create a title that combines Style 1 and Style 2 for an essay beginning with the second sample introductory paragraph.

Exercise 4.5 C

1. Create a title in Style 1 for an essay beginning with the introductory paragraph you wrote for Exercise 4.2 C, question 1.

2. Create a title in Style 2 for an essay beginning with the introductory paragraph you wrote for Exercise 4.2 C, question 1.

3. Create a title that combines Style 1 and Style 2 for an essay beginning with the introductory paragraph you wrote for Exercise 4.

\\ CLOSE READINGS

Close reading is an approach to literary analysis that pays careful attention to the language in a passage or a complete short text such as a poem. **Close readings usually proceed line by line through a text, noting and analyzing important words, phrases, literary devices, and so on.** (A parallel technique can be used to analyze an image or a series of images, such as a short scene from a film.) A close reading is often a preliminary step toward an essay that considers the significance of a passage in relation to an entire work—a passage analysis essay. It can also be the start of the writing process when a poem or other short text is the subject of an essay. Instructors sometimes require students to complete close readings as assignments in themselves.

A close reading may focus on a text that is marked by an unusual vocabulary and packed with complicated figurative language, but it is often rewarding to look carefully at passages in which the language does not, at first, draw attention to itself. Examples in this section are based on the seemingly simple first two lines of "Anecdote of the Jar," by Wallace Stevens: "I placed a jar in Tennessee, / And round it was, upon a hill" (1–2). The poem was first published in 1923. The complete poem can be found on pages 95. (Exercise 2.4 offers some examples of close analysis of figurative language and sense images.)

It helps to think of a close reading as involving a series of five steps:

1. **Paraphrase the literal content.** Before you can understand the significance of a particular word choice, or a pattern in sentence structure, or an unusual **trope**[1], you need to know what the text means in the simplest, most obvious sense. Who is/ are the narrator(s) or speaker(s)? What is she or he talking about, and to whom? If the text is a passage in a longer work, situate the passage in relation to the rest of the work (near the beginning, in the middle, at the beginning of the third act of a play, etc.). To make sure that you understand, paraphrase the literal meaning of the text in one or two sentences, and, if it is part of a longer work, specify its place in that work.

---

[1] For brief definitions of bolded literary terms and some advice on how to use them in your analyses, see Appendix 5: Glossary of Literary Terms.

2. **Example:** The passage contains the first two lines of a twelve-line poem. The speaker, an unspecified person, says that he put a round jar on a hill in Tennessee, which is a state in the southeastern United States. The speaker does not specify an audience being addressed.

3. **Identify significant words, phrases, and formal features.** It takes practice to be able to identify with confidence the details that matter. It helps to proceed through a checklist. The following list of things to note is not complete (creating a truly exhaustive list would be impossible), but it will give you a starting point for a close reading.

    1. Figurative language
    2. Sense imagery
    3. Literary or historical allusions
    4. Repetition of words or phrases
    5. Unusual words or phrases
    6. Symbols
    7. Puns
    8. Rhyme
    9. Alliteration
    10. Metre

    Example: The two lines contain no clear examples of figurative language, sense images, puns, rhyme, or alliteration. There are no strikingly unusual words. The word "place" is slightly formal, when considered in contrast with "put," the obvious alternative, as is "upon" in contrast with "on." The word "Tennessee" is not unusual by itself, but it is unusual to speak of placing a small object such as a jar in an area as large as a state. One usually speaks of "placing" such an object on a shelf, or on a table, etc. The attention drawn to the jar suggests that it is a symbol. The Appalachian Mountains cover eastern Tennessee, and the region is sometimes referred to as the Tennessee Hills. Since the jar is placed on a hill, it may be that the speaker is referring to the Appalachian region of the state (although there are, obviously, hills elsewhere in Tennessee). There is no internal or end rhyme. There is a regular metre: iambic tetrameter.

4. **Describe the sentences and sentence structures.** Specify whether each sentence is short or long, and whether it is simple, compound, or complex. Are the sentences questions or statements? Are there any sentence fragments or run-on sentences? Is there anything unusual in the **syntax** throughout the passage?

    Example: The two lines contain one declarative compound sentence, with each line consisting of one clause. The syntax of the second clause is unusual. It would be more common in contemporary English, and in the English of the time when the poem was written, to put the word "round" after "was": "and it was round." The syntax of "round it was" has an old-fashioned quality, even suggestive of biblical English. Also, the way in which the phrase "upon a hill" is linked to the first part of the sentence is odd. The sentence suggests that the roundness of the jar somehow *occurs* on the hill. If the jar is round, it would be round anywhere, so it is odd to say that it is round "upon a hill."

5. **Identify significant patterns in the manner of expression, along with exceptions to those patterns.** Review your results from steps 2 and 3, and ask yourself questions that will lead you to generalize about the language of the passage or text. Is the text marked by figurative language? Is it a series of questions? Is the language generally formal and technically correct, or is it casual and conversational? Is the vocabulary drawn from a particular profession or subculture? Are there words, phrases, or sentences that stand out because they vary in some way from the rest of the text?

    Example: The language is not obviously unusual. The words are short and common. Each line has an unusual quality, the first because of the strangeness of the idea of putting a jar in an area as large as a state, and the second because of its unconventional syntax. A few slightly formal words, as noted above, give the entire passage a formal quality.

6. **Make observations about the significance of the details and patterns you have identified.** Think of all of the elements of the passage that you have noted as evidence. The evidence may suggest important things about the personality, attitudes, thoughts, mood, education, class, culture, or other characteristics of the speaker or narrator, or of other characters. The evidence may also imply important things about the world in which the text is set. Note whether the language draws attention to concrete things in a way that suggests they should be understood as symbols. Be particularly alert to the potential for the evidence you have discovered to suggest ideas that contradict or complicate things being expressed on a literal level.

    Example: As suggested by the slightly formal quality of the language and also by the regular metre, the speaker seems to be careful or even a bit fastidious. There is a lot of room in an entire state for an object the size of a jar, but the word "place" conveys the sense that even with all of this room, the speaker is still taking care about the positioning of the jar. The care he or she takes suggests that the action is important. Though the language is not highly technical, it is grammatically correct, and this correctness also suggests a careful quality in the speaker.

    The unusual syntax in the second line, particularly in the biblical syntax of the phrase "And round it was" gives the passage a religious tone. Together with the odd picture of a person carefully placing a jar within a state, on a hill, the impression conveyed is almost that of a religious ritual being undertaken, with the jar a religious symbol. The second line gives the impression that the speaker, after placing the jar, is standing back and observing it in a way that makes the jar seem important.

The mountainous region of eastern Tennessee has long been presented in popular American culture as having a wild, lawless quality, and the speaker's specifying of a "hill" in Tennessee invites associations with this region, through the connection to the Tennessee Hills and the related derogatory term "hillbilly," which had entered the language by the time the poem was written. The persona of the careful, fastidious, correct speaker contrasts with the negative stereotype of the people who live in the area: the ill-mannered, uneducated hillbillies.

\\ PASSAGE ANALYSIS ESSAYS

A common assignment for students is the passage analysis essay, which is related to close reading as it focuses on a single passage from a literary text. The assignment encourages students to analyze details, such as individual words and phrases, as all the evidence must be drawn from a small section of text. It also encourages students to make connections between details and the meaning of the text, as **the analysis does not treat the passage as a complete text in itself, but as a part of a whole**. The assignment helps students to overcome a problem that sometimes arises: the tendency to summarize plots rather than analyze.

Passage analysis essays are often assigned in exam situations, in most cases with the students not knowing ahead of time what passage will be selected for them. **The best way to prepare for such assignments is to replicate the conditions on your own.** Select different passages from the literary texts you might be asked to analyze. Write several practice essays using these passages. Review your essays afterward, noting whether your analysis has been structured successfully and how it can be improved. If you have a confident understanding of the structure your essay will follow, you will be freer in the exam situation to reflect on the passage and develop your insights.

INTRODUCTIONS TO PASSAGE ANALYSIS ESSAYS

Introductions to passage analysis essays follow the structure of introductory paragraphs described in Chapter 4 (see pages 48–49). In the section in which the evidence is previewed, the "evidence" is the passage to be analyzed, which should be referred to by summarizing its content (not by providing its page number, and not by quoting it).

Sample Introductory Paragraph: Passage Analysis Essay

The following paragraph is a sample introduction for an essay focusing on a single passage (a simple version):

Raymond Carver's "The Bridle" is about freedom and materialism. In a key passage in the story, the narrator, Marge, describes a party that she goes to with Harley. The passage makes an important contribution to one of the story's main themes, the theme that materialism is bad because it limits people's freedom.

Here is a more ambitious sample introduction for an essay focusing on a single passage:

"The Bridle," by Raymond Carver, is a complex study of freedom and materialism. In a key passage in the story, the narrator, Marge, describes a party that she attends with Harley. The party dramatizes the way in which the lives of the story's characters are constrained by their own diminishing expectations of themselves and each other, in such a way as to suggest that the problems faced by Marge are not hers alone but are connected to a force in her society. The story argues that this force is materialism, and that although a society given over to materialism may offer the illusion of freedom, it in fact denies people the opportunity to make the kinds of commitments to each other that are necessary to be truly free.

THE STRUCTURE OF PASSAGE ANALYSIS ESSAYS

The structure of passage analysis essays is not very different from that of essays that consider more evidence. While other essays may take evidence from anywhere in the text, the passage analysis essay uses analytical claims that refer to the passage alone, and the evidence must come from that passage. The final body paragraph is an exception to this structure. The final body paragraph begins with a claim about the resolution of the conflict (this is almost always the case in essays dealing with drama or prose fiction) or about crucial evidence that establishes the attitude of the text to the issues it represents. The final analysis applies the understanding gained through the analysis of the passage.

One of the problems students have in writing passage analysis essays is a tendency to treat the passage as though it is a complete literary text that expresses a theme. **Remember that the passage itself does not express a theme.** It reveals things that contribute to an understanding of what is represented by the whole text.

WORKING WITH PASSAGE ANALYSIS ESSAYS

The following thesis and claims are taken from the sample passage analysis essay in Appendix 2 (see page 106).

Thesis: The passage makes an important contribution to the story's theme, which is that even if a minority culture is characterized by peace and love, its most powerful representative cannot change an unjust society.

Claim 1: The passage suggests that Gerry's size represents his power, and this size is shown to contrast with the weighshack, and, therefore, with the society he is immersed in.

Claim 2: Through the description of the skill with which Gerry disarms Dot, the passage emphasizes the depth of his power, which is almost magical.

Claim 3:   The way in which Gerry takes the knitting needles from Dot and his compliment on her work reveal Gerry's peaceful, loving nature.

Claim 4:   The resolution of the conflict, in which Jason, the child of Dot and Gerry, is placed on the scale with monumental hope, but no effect, suggests that even a powerful minority that is peaceful and loving cannot bring about change in an unjust society.

KEY POINTS

- Before beginning a close reading, paraphrase the literal content of the text.
- Close readings proceed line by line.
- Passage analysis essays focus on a single passage from a text, but they do not treat the passage as a complete text in itself. They connect the passage to the whole text.

EXERCISE SET 5.1—UNDERSTANDING PASSAGE ANALYSIS ESSAY STRUCTURE

Exercise 5.1 A (Answers are in Appendix 4)

1. Identify the key words in the thesis of the passage analysis essay above.
2. Identify the words in Claim 1 that repeat key words in the thesis.
3. Identify the words in Claim 2 that repeat key words in the thesis.
4. From what part of the story is the evidence for Claim 1 taken?
5. From what part of the story is the evidence for Claim 2 taken?

Exercise 5.1 B

1. Identify the key words in Claim 4 that repeat key words in the thesis.
2. From what part of the story is the evidence for Claim 3 taken?
3. From what part of the story is the evidence for Claim 4 taken?

Exercise 5.1 C

1. Choose what you think is an interesting passage of about ten lines from a literary text that you have been studying in class. Make a list of the elements of

literature that you have studied (for example, symbols and figures of speech). Identify any examples in the passage.

2. Write several sentences about what the passage reveals or suggests about anything significant in the literary text, including characters, setting, the society or community in which the story takes place, important objects, or important events. Pay close attention to the literary elements you identified in your answer to question 1.

3. Review your answer to question 2 and make notes about the connections between the things you observed and a main conflict or an important issue in the literary text. (Perhaps the passage reveals something about a character who is involved in a main conflict, or about natural or social forces that are part of a conflict, or about the text's attitude toward a character or an idea.)

4. Carefully reread the section of the literary text in which the conflict is resolved, or those key parts of the text that establish its attitude to the ideas represented. Make notes on how you can apply the understanding of the passage that you developed in the previous questions to an analysis of the resolution, or, in the case of a short poem, to an analysis of the work as a whole.

5. Write an outline for an essay analyzing the passage. Make sure that each analytical claim up to the last focuses on something revealed by the passage. The final analytical claim must state something about the resolution of the conflict or, in the case of a short poem, about the attitude expressed by the text.

\\ COMPARATIVE LITERARY ANALYSIS ESSAYS

THE PURPOSE OF COMPARATIVE LITERARY ANALYSIS ESSAYS

Comparative essays analyze more than one literary text at a time. The texts may be of different genres, such as a novel and a film. Such essays draw attention to similarities and differences between texts in order to illuminate features of both that might otherwise not be evident. For example, if you analyze two texts whose themes have to do with the importance of independence, the comparison may bring to light subtle differences in their respective ideas about independence, differences that we might not otherwise notice. As well, texts that seem to be very different may, when compared, reveal interesting parallels that point to similar meanings that we might otherwise miss.

A danger with comparative essays is that they can easily become lists of similarities and differences. Another danger is that they can become separate arguments about different texts, simply merged into a single document. **There must be a reason to consider** the two or more texts you are looking at in a single essay, and that reason must be made clear to the reader.

Unless you have been specifically instructed to do so, do not comment on which of your selected texts you think is better. As with essays on a single literary text, your audience is interested in the ideas the texts express, not in your evaluation of them.

INTRODUCTIONS TO COMPARATIVE LITERARY ANALYSIS ESSAYS

Introductions to comparative literary analysis essays follow the same structure as literary analysis essays that deal with only one text, but there is a doubling up (or tripling, etc.) in each element of the paragraph. There is also a statement that specifies a key difference or similarity.

SAMPLE INTRODUCTORY PARAGRAPH: COMPARATIVE LITERARY ANALYSIS ESSAY

Alex B. Rankin's novel *Brilliantine* and Davinder Lee's novel *Of Arrangements* are both about the destructive effects of the illusion of love. While the two novels may seem to be dramatizing similar notions about the damage we do by believing in love's reality, considering the texts together reveals a subtle but important contrast in what they imply about the significance of the unreality of love. Through the depiction of characters who seek an alternative to love, *Brilliantine* suggests that we can reject the illusion of love and still bring meaning into our lives and our cultures, while *Of Arrangements*, by depicting characters who reject love, makes the bleak argument that other attempts to find meaning are just as illusory.

THE STRUCTURE OF COMPARATIVE LITERARY ANALYSIS ESSAYS

There are two basic structures for comparative essays. Structure 1 presents a complete argument about one text, followed by a parallel, complete argument about a second text. The second section consistently refers back to the first, elaborating on similarities and differences. Structure 2 alternates between the texts, usually presenting one paragraph on one text and then another, parallel paragraph on the second text. Essays written by first- and second-year English literature students are usually brief; in such essays this alternating between texts should be carried through to the conclusion, in the same order in which the texts are mentioned in the introductory paragraph. In longer essays, the structure can vary when appropriate. Sometimes several paragraphs will discuss one text, followed by several paragraphs on another. Transitional paragraphs are useful in such essays, which can become confusing without them.

- The reason you are considering two or more texts must be made clear to the reader.

- Use transitional paragraphs between sections that discuss different texts.

WORKING WITH COMPARATIVE LITERARY ANALYSIS ESSAYS
Sample outline: Comparative Literary Analysis Essay (Structure 2)

Thesis: Through its depiction of those characters who seek an alternative to love, *Brilliantine* suggests that we can find other ways to bring meaning into our lives and our cultures that are more honest and fulfilling, while *Of Arrangements*, also through the depictions of the characters who reject love, makes the bleak argument that any attempt to centre ourselves or our cultures leads us to accept illusions that undermine our lives.

Claim 1:   In *Brilliantine*, David's commitment to art and Susan's developing religious faith are presented as alternatives to love.

Claim 2:   In *Of Arrangements*, in a manner quite similar to the way in which David and Susan function in *Brilliantine*, the entire Stasny family represents the rejection of love and the search for alternatives, including religion, art, and power over others.

Claim 3:   Though David does not succeed as an artist, *Brilliantine* suggests that even in his failure there is a fundamental honesty that is valuable in itself and unavailable to those who believe in love.

Claim 4:   The artists in the Stasny family, in contrast with *Brilliantine*'s David, reveal themselves to be just as self-deceptive and, therefore, unfulfilled as the more major characters who believe in love.

Claim 5:   Through Susan's religious faith, the resolution of *Brilliantine* suggests that there is a way to make our lives and the cultures of which we are a part meaningful, if we can honestly come to understand our desires as being important only in connection to something greater than ourselves.

Claim 6:   Though the religious daughter and the power-seeking son in *Of Arrangements* seem satisfied and even happy by the novel's conclusion, the narrator's descriptions of important symbols in the final scene suggest that this positive picture is an illusion, and that any attempt we make to find a centre of value in our lives is doomed to undermine itself.

EXERCISE SET 5.2—UNDERSTANDING COMPARATIVE LITERARY ANALYSIS ESSAYS

Exercise 5.2 A (Answers are in Appendix 4)

1. Identify the five components of the sample introductory paragraph for the comparative literary analysis essay.

2. Identify the key words in the first sentence of the introduction.

3. Identify the words in the thesis that repeat key words from the introduction's first sentence (the words may be in slightly different form).

Exercise 5.2 B

1. Identify the words in the claims of the sample outline that repeat key words in the thesis.

Exercise 5.2 C

1. Identify two literary texts that you have been studying that are about similar abstract topics. Write an introduction for a comparative literary analysis essay that points out their important similarity and concludes with a thesis that addresses the contrast in their themes.

2. Identify two literary texts that you have been studying that are about different abstract topics. Write an introduction for a comparative literary analysis essay that points out their difference and concludes with a thesis that addresses their surprising thematic similarity.

3. Write an outline for a comparative literary analysis essay, using the thesis you wrote in answer to question 1.

4. Write an outline for a comparative literary analysis essay, using the thesis you wrote in answer to question 2.

\\ LITERARY ANALYSIS RESEARCH ESSAYS

LITERARY ANALYSIS RESEARCH ESSAYS USING CRITICAL SOURCES

The Purpose of Critical Sources

Literary analysis research essays use the work of other literary critics, called critical sources, to establish the relationship between what the writer of the essay states and what others have said on the same or related topics. When professors write literary analysis essays, they need to review much—frequently all—of what has been written on their topic. They then need to establish carefully that what they have to say is new, and how exactly it fits in with what others have said; readers are not interested in an essay that presents an idea that they have already encountered. Students do not need to review all of the material published on the text they are analyzing, or even most of it, but at a certain point, your instructors will expect you to look at some critical sources and to say something about your argument in relation to those sources.

Critical sources are not used to prove your argument. Students sometimes look at what critics have written in the hope of finding out the "truth" about the text they are analyzing. The important evidence in a literary analysis research essay must still come from the text that you analyze, and the important things that are said about that evidence—the analysis—must be your ideas.

FINDING CRITICAL SOURCES

Research can be difficult, confusing, and time consuming. Before you begin, it is best to have a simple strategy in mind. The two main sources for critical work in English literature are books and articles, and there are some steps to follow when looking for each, as well as for using specialized reference works and the Internet. If you lack experience in library research, try to find a time when the library is not busy, so that it is more likely that a reference librarian will be available to help you. You will find that reference librarians in academic libraries are highly expert and very helpful when you get stuck in your research. If your library offers tutorial sessions, take advantage of them. A short period of instruction from a librarian on the specifics of research in your library can save you countless hours.

BOOKS   Find books by searching your library catalogue by subject. Begin with the title of the text you are analyzing and move to more general topics until you have success. If you are writing a critical research essay on a poem or a short story, for example, it is likely that you will not find any books specifically on that work. The next logical step would be to search for books on the author. Be sure to search for the author as a subject, not as author. You want to find books *about* the author's literary texts, not those *by* the author of the literary text.

You may find that there are many books on the author whose text you are analyzing, so many that it is overwhelming. The catalogue will divide the books up into categories, and you can narrow the choice by focusing on the category of "Interpretation and Criticism." If, however, there are only a few books, and some are in the category of "Biography," do not ignore them. Biographies sometimes include substantial amounts of valuable literary criticism. The titles of the books and information that the catalogue offers regarding the contents of each book can also help you to decide which will be most likely to be useful to you. The catalogue should indicate whether or not each book has an index, and if you have many books to choose from you should consider ignoring the ones without indexes. It is unlikely that you will have the time to read whole books when looking for a few comments relevant to your topic, and you can use indexes to guide you to relevant sections. Note that indexes of books on a single author sometimes list the different texts discussed, not individually by title, but in a list under the heading "Works," or under the heading of the author's last name, then "Works."

You may also find the opposite problem: instead of being overwhelmed by the number of books on an author or literary text, you might find none at all. In this case, you need to broaden your search. Instead of looking for works specifically on your author, look for those on categories of literature that correspond to your author or the specific text. Suppose, for example, that you are writing an essay on Charlotte Perkins Gilman's "The Yellow Wallpaper," and you can find no books, or very few, on the story or on Gilman. Search for books on the American short story, on women American writers, on American literature of the nineteenth century, on feminist literature of the nineteenth century, and so on. You should be able to find several books on categories of literature in which "The Yellow Wallpaper" can be placed, and when you consult their indexes you may find specific references to the story. Even if you can find no specific references to the story or to Gilman, you may be able to make use of critics' more general comments about literature of a certain type or period.

Bibliographies and notes in books, as well as in articles, can offer valuable suggestions about other sources. Noting which texts are frequently cited by other critics also helps identify important criticism.

ARTICLES   You can search for articles using strategies that are roughly similar to those you use to find books. The articles you will find useful are published in academic journals that are indexed and made available through computerized databases. Your library will likely subscribe to some of these databases (they are not usually free), and you will be able to use them to search for articles on your topic. Again, begin with specific searches and move to more general ones till you have success. Some articles will be available only in journals to which your institution does not subscribe, and unless you are doing research at an advanced level and have a lot of time, you should simply skip to those articles that are available through your institution. Some articles will be available in their entirety online, and you will be able to print them out on the spot. For others, you will need to track down the print edition of the journal in which the article appears. The listing in the database will give you all the information you need to find the journal, the specific issue of the journal, and the article.

Articles have the advantage of being very specific. **You are much more likely to find an article on a single poem or story than an entire book on the same text.** A potential disadvantage is the difficulty of some articles. You are likely to find some articles hard to understand. It can even seem that they are written in a strange dialect of English. Do not be discouraged or feel that the problem lies with you. If you persist, you will find articles that, though challenging, can be helpful if read patiently. If you continue in English literature, your ability to make use of scholarly articles will improve, and you will also develop a sense of which journals tend to publish more clearly written work. Searching in databases for articles can be a bit confusing. Remember to ask a librarian to help you if you get stuck. Because of the importance of articles and because of the initial difficulties in searching for them, academic libraries frequently offer specific tutorial sessions on finding articles.

SPECIALIZED REFERENCE WORKS   Before beginning to look for books or articles, consider consulting some specialized reference works to get an introduction to the literary text you are working on and its author. There are dictionaries, encyclopedias, and similar works that focus on literature written in certain periods and by the writers of certain nations, and on other relevant categories. You will find these books in the reference section of the library. The information you will find can help you to create effective searches when looking for books and articles. A short entry in a reference work might, for example, tell you that the author whose play you are studying was a Catholic. If you searched your catalogue for a book using the terms "Catholicism" and "Literature" you might find a general work that included a discussion of the writer or even the specific text you are studying.

Avoid relying only on specialized reference works for the information you include in your research essays. Your instructor will usually expect more specific information from articles and books.

THE INTERNET   There is a lot of useful information available on the Internet, but very little that is of use to you in your academic work, with the exception of articles that are sometimes available after first being published in academic journals. Google searches and resources such as Wikipedia can be tempting, but if you begin your search there, recognize that you will eventually need to move on to reliable scholarly sources. You are likely to come across much unreliable work that will only detract from your success. While Internet searches can sometimes link you to an academic journal's website, often you will have to pay a fee to access the full article, whereas you can probably retrieve it for free from your school library's database.

KEY POINTS

- Do not use critical sources to prove your argument.

- When you cannot find works specifically on your author, look for those on categories of literature that correspond to your author or the specific text.

- If you get stuck in your research, consider asking a librarian for help.

PLAGIARISM

If you use someone else's words or ideas in an essay without being clear that you are doing so, you are plagiarizing. Plagiarism is a serious academic offence. In most academic institutions, the penalties for it are severe. When writing a literary analysis essay, if you express an idea about a literary text, or point out that certain evidence is important, or explain the implicit meaning of a passage, or if you make a claim about the significance of an entire text or a body of texts, your readers assume that the words and ideas they are reading originate with you. If their assumption is incorrect because you have not credited the source of the words or ideas, you have plagiarized. When you use words and ideas from other sources, avoid plagiarism by paraphrasing, summarizing, or quoting, and by citing the sources.

Examples in this section are based on the following passage from *Rainforest Narratives: The Work of Janette Turner Hospital*, by David Callahan. Callahan is analyzing Hospital's novel *Orpheus Lost*:

> Leela and Mishka are connected in terms of their mirrored obsessions, given that Leela is a mathematician, her special area of research the mathematics of music. Music and mathematics are intimately linked via their investment in measurable patterns, systems and the pleasures of arranging the units of their respective notational codes. (291)

PARAPHRASING   To paraphrase is to rewrite a brief passage in your own words. Changing the word order a bit, or altering the form of words, does not constitute proper paraphrase. If you find that you have difficulty expressing the ideas of a specific passage in your own words, quote instead of paraphrasing.

Paraphrase:
David Callahan observes that music and mathematics are very similar, in that they both involve patterns and systems (291).

> **Correct:**   The sentence paraphrases the first sentence of the passage from Callahan's book. Though the words "music," "mathematics," "patterns," and "systems" are taken from the source, they are not special terms or original phrases that themselves express Callahan's ideas. Using them in this way does not give a misleading impression that the specific way of expressing an idea is yours rather than Callahan's.

Plagiarism: Paraphrase that includes unacknowledged quotation
David Callahan observes that Leela and Mishka are connected to each other through their mirrored obsessions, music and mathematics, which have an intimate link (291).

Incorrect:	Callahan is cited, but one phrase from the original passage, "mirrored obsessions" is repeated without being enclosed within quotation marks. The term "mirrored," in particular, specifying the relationship between the obsessions, constitutes one of Callahan's insights, so it needs to be credited. Similarly, the phrase "have an intimate link" is too close to the phrasing of the original ("are intimately linked,") and gives a false impression that the language is not Callahan's.

PLAGIARISM: PARAPHRASE WITHOUT CITATION

Music and mathematics are very similar, in that they both involve patterns and systems.

Incorrect:	The idea is Callahan's, but Callahan is not cited.

Summarizing

To summarize is to condense a longer passage by presenting its main idea or ideas, again using your own words. If you have difficulty using your own words, try taking point-form notes from the passage (or even an entire article or book) that you are summarizing. Write your summary while referring to your notes rather than to the original text. If there are key phrases and terms in the source text that must be repeated, use quotation marks.

Summary:
David Callahan notes the commonality between music and mathematics, and the way in which Leela and Mishka's interest in them establishes an important connection between the two characters.

Correct:	Callaghan's main idea is condensed and presented in the writer's own words. Page numbers are not provided here because the entire work is being summarized.

Plagiarism: Summary with unacknowledged quotation

David Callahan explains the intimate link between music and mathematics, and the way in which Leela and Mishka are connected to each other through their mirrored obsessions with one of these fields.

Incorrect:	The summary uses key words and phrases from the original without quotation marks and without an appropriate citation.

Quoting

To quote is to reproduce the words of the original. Integrate the quotations so as to keep changes to the original to a minimum, and if you do make small changes, indicate that you have done so with square brackets. Every phrase taken directly from the original is enclosed within quotation marks.

Quotation:

David Callahan argues that "Leela and Mishka are connected in terms of their mirrored obsessions" with music and mathematics, which are similar because they both involve "measurable patterns, systems and the pleasures of arranging the units of their respective notational codes" (291).

> **Correct:** The writer's use of quotation marks clearly distinguishes between the writer's own words and Callahan's.

Plagiarism: Incomplete use of quotation marks

According to David Callahan, "Leela and Mishka are connected in terms of their mirrored obsessions" with music and mathematics (291). Their interests connect them because music and mathematics are themselves connected through the importance they place on measurable patterns and arranging the units of their notational codes.

> *Incorrect:* The second sentence copies wording from the source without using quotation marks.

If you have doubts about whether something you write should be attributed to a source or not, always check with your instructor.

Tutors and Academic Integrity

A problem that is not technically plagiarism, but that involves similar issues, can arise when students use tutors. If you use a tutor to help you with an essay, whether the tutor is a professional or just a fellow student giving you some advice, you need to make sure that the words and ideas remain yours. Tutors can point out parts of your essay that are unclear or confusing and can help you to discover more effective ways of structuring your ideas. They can identify common writing problems you might have and assist you in identifying and correcting those problems.

Do not use a tutor to supply phrases, words, or ideas, or to proofread or edit your work. The ideas and words, including the grammar and punctuation, must remain yours. Students may be found guilty of cheating when the essays they write at home are much more effectively written than those done in class. Instructors expect the essays students write at home to be more polished, but when the difference is too extreme, that difference can be taken as proof that a student has used a tutor illegitimately.

KEY POINTS

- Avoid plagiarism by paraphrasing, summarizing, or quoting, and by citing the sources.

- If you have doubts about whether something you write should be attributed to a source or not, ask your instructor.

- Tutors should not provide you witty phrases, words, or ideas, and they should not proofread or edit your work.

Uses for Critical Sources

This section lists four ways to use information from critical sources to build or support an argument. Make sure you know the exact purpose of any critical source you use in your essay. Remember that the critical source does not prove your argument. (Exercise Set 5.3 will help you use a sample essay to find examples of the uses for critical sources.)

1. **General statements by critics can be used to establish the background of a more specific claim that you want to make.** If, for example, you are analyzing a symbol in a text, you can cite a critic who says that the text is highly symbolic. You can also cite a more general claim that the author writes symbolically, not just in the text you are analyzing. The critical source makes it clear that your argument is consistent with the way some critics think about your author. Your task will still be to present evidence from the text to support your argument about the specific symbol.

2. **Statements by critics can be extended to apply to texts or features of texts to which the statements do not refer directly.** For example, a critic might comment about a theme, setting, or character, in a certain text. You can cite that comment when analyzing a similar theme, setting, or character in a different text by the same author. The critical source is used to show that your analysis is broadening the reach of the critic's argument to include new material. The consistency between your claim and that of the critic does not prove that your claim is true; the proof still needs to come from the literary text that you analyze.

3. **Statements by critics can be disagreed with and argued against in your essay.** A critic might argue that the text presents a certain character as entirely negative, while you believe that the character is a mix of negative and positive. Citing the critic establishes that what you are stating is controversial and, therefore, worth

supporting with detailed analysis. You might find that what a critic argues about one text by an author does not apply to a different text. In this case, the critic is worth citing in order to show that your analysis establishes a certain range or variety in the author's work. In all cases in which you disagree with critics, the disagreement is worth noting because it suggests that your analysis is new. Note that your disagreement must be polite and respectful. Insulting critics with whom you disagree does not strengthen your argument.

4. **General statements by critics can be applied to your specific argument.** Such statements are used to establish the relationship of your argument about a specific literary text to what is thought about other texts of a similar kind. If the critic's general statement is consistent with your specific analysis, it can be used to reinforce the general credibility of your approach. For example, the comment that much Canadian literature of the mid-twentieth century is concerned with the idea of community could be used to justify a consideration of the idea of community in a Canadian poem written in that period. If your specific analysis is inconsistent with the general statement, you can use that statement to show that your position is worth developing in detail to show that the literary text in question is an exception. If, for example, a critic says that the protagonists of early American novels are **allegorical** rather than realistic, the comment would be worth quoting in an essay that treats such a protagonist as a realistic figure. You can include statements that apply to the genre of the text and the period in which it is written, as well as to literature produced by writers of the same nation, class, gender, ideology, or culture.

KEY POINTS

- Make sure that you understand why you are using a critical source and that you make that purpose clear to your readers.

INTRODUCTIONS TO LITERARY ANALYSIS RESEARCH ESSAYS USING CRITICAL SOURCES

If what the critics have to say about the text you are analyzing is relevant to the evidence that you focus on generally in your essay, or to your thesis, it is helpful to refer to their comments in the introduction. Doing so establishes right away what the relationship is between your analysis and theirs. Note that critical sources can be incorporated into all kinds of literary analysis essays, including essays that compare two or more works and those that focus on a single passage.

WORKING WITH CRITICAL SOURCES

Sample Introductory Paragraph: Literary Analysis Research Essay Using Critical Sources

Davinder Lee's novel *Of Arrangements* is a complex text that dramatizes problems in modern culture. At least two critics agree that the problem at the centre of the novel is the illusion of modern love. Seamus E. Elliott argues that the source of the illusion that the protagonists, Hai and Jefferson, succumb to is their shared obsession with Hollywood romantic comedy (74–84), and Sally Franklin argues that the reason their judgments about others are so inaccurate is the influence of this shallow, illusory idea of love (112–15). Both critics agree that the disastrous fate of the characters implies a criticism of modern love (Elliott 223–36; Franklin 337–40). The logic of these analyses of the protagonists and what is represented by their fates also applies to several minor characters, especially the members of the Stasny family. When these characters are examined carefully, it becomes apparent that *Of Arrangements* not only criticizes modern ideas of love; it also makes the bleak argument that any attempt to make our lives meaningful leads us to accept illusions that undermine our lives.

You may find that the critics' comments that are useful to you do not relate directly to what you say in your introduction. If so, simply include the comments where relevant in your analytical paragraphs.

EXERCISE SET 5.3—UNDERSTANDING THE USE OF CRITICAL SOURCES

Exercise 5.3 A (Answers are in Appendix 4)

1. What is the function of the critical sources referred to in the sample introduction?
2. What is the function of the critical source referred to in the introduction to the literary analysis research essay using critical sources in Appendix 2 (page 112)?
3. What is the function of the critical source referred to in the third body paragraph of the essay referred to in question 2?

Exercise 5.3 B

1. What is the function of the critical source referred to in the fourth body paragraph of the literary analysis research essay using critical sources in Appendix 2 (page 113)?
2. What is the function of the critical source referred to in the seventh body paragraph of the essay referred to in question 1?

Exercise 5.3 C

1. Find a critical source that makes a general comment about some feature or quality of a category of literature in which the literary text you have been working with in previous exercises could be placed (for example, American literature, literature written by women in the nineteenth century, or the sonnet). On an index card, a piece of paper, or a word processing document, record the exact wording of the comment, in quotation marks. Record all the publication information that would need to be included on your Works Cited page. (See Appendix 1 for a brief discussion of the Works Cited page.)

2. On the same document in which you recorded your answer to question 1, paraphrase the critic's comment in your own words.

3. On the same document, note whether you think the critic's comment applies to the literary text you are analyzing, or whether that text is an exception to the comment.

4. Find a critical source that makes a general comment about the collective body of work of the author of the literary text you are analyzing. On an index card, piece of paper, or word-processing document, write down the exact wording of the comment, in quotation marks. Record all the publication information that would need to be included in your Works Cited list.

5. On the same document on which you recorded your answer to question 4, paraphrase the critic's comment.

6. On the same document, note whether you think the critic's comment applies to the literary text you are analyzing, or whether that text is an exception to the comment.

7. Find a critical source that makes a comment about the abstract topic or the theme of the literary text you are analyzing. On an index card, a piece of paper, or a word-processing document, write down the exact wording of the comment, in quotation marks. Record all the publication information that would need to be included on your Works Cited page.

8. On the same document on which you recorded your answer to question 7, paraphrase the critic's comment.

9. On the same document, note whether the abstract topic or theme the critic identifies is different from what you have found in the literary text that you are analyzing.

10. Write an introductory paragraph for an essay on the literary text that you have been analyzing, including a reference to one of the critical sources quoted in your previous answers. In a separate short paragraph, explain the function of the critical source.

11. Write an analytical paragraph on the literary text that you have been analyzing, including a reference to one of the critical sources quoted in your previous answers. In a separate short paragraph, explain the function of the critical source.

LITERARY ANALYSIS RESEARCH ESSAYS USING HISTORICAL SOURCES

The Purpose Of Historical Sources

Literary texts are not written in a vacuum; they are written in and often set in specific places and times. **It is frequently crucial to know something about these historical contexts in order to make convincing arguments about what texts mean.** Historical sources provide important information about the context of literary texts, information that contributes to an analysis. In some cases, these sources are original documents, but in most student essays the sources are books or articles written by historians.

In order to know what the relevant historical context is, you will probably have to do some research. You need to find out when and where the literary text you are working on was written, as well as when and where it is set. (The difference between the two contexts can be crucial to your analysis. An allegorical poem set in biblical times, for example, may become more meaningful when you consider the politics of the time in which it was written, during the Restoration, for example.) You can then develop questions about the historical context of the text that might lead to information that will contribute to your analysis.

As with critical sources, **historical sources do not prove things about texts.** If a historian says that the late 1960s was a time of rebellion, this statement does not prove that a poem written in that era expresses rebellious ideas. The important evidence must come from the literary text, and the analysis must focus on the evidence.

Uses For Historical Sources

This section lists three ways to use information from historical sources in your essays. (Exercise Set 5.4 will help you use a sample essay to find examples of the uses for historical sources.)

1. **Historical sources can help reveal the significance of small details in a text that we might otherwise overlook.** For example, if a man in a short story has long hair, the significance of that particular fashion choice would depend on the era in which the story is set. In one period, it might suggest that the man likes classical music and thinks of himself as an intellectual, while in another, it might suggest that he opposes the Vietnam War or, more generally, the values of his parents' generation.

2. **Historical sources can explain the distinguishing attitudes and values of a culture, what can be called its *ethos*, which may be crucial for understanding**

the significance of specific details in a text as well as more general issues. For example, we cannot know if the values of a character represent the values of her culture unless we know something about that culture. If a poem describes a woman leaving her husband, whether her doing so suggests she is a daring rebel or not depends in part on the attitude of her culture toward women and marriage. Historical research can help answer such questions.

3. **Historical sources can explain the significance of events or social developments that may shape our understanding of literary texts.** If a poem is written soon after World War One, it may be useful to know what the effect of the war was on the attitudes of people at that time, attitudes to matters as diverse as the existence of God, the purpose of art, and so on. When literary texts allude to historical events, what those allusions mean depends on the significance of the events, and, again, historical research is frequently needed to discover what that significance is. Sometimes it is very clear that we need to know something about historical context in order to understand a text. It would be difficult, for example, to imagine someone making a convincing analysis of Toni Morrison's *Beloved* without knowing something about the history of slavery in the United States.

Introductions For Literary Analysis Research Essays Using Historical Sources

Introductions for literary analysis research essays using historical sources follow the same structure as that of introductory paragraphs for essays not using such sources. If the historical context is an important enough feature of a part of your analysis, include a reference to it in the middle section of the paragraph.

KEY POINTS

- It is often important to have an understanding of a text's historical in order to make a convincing argument about what the text means.

WORKING WITH HISTORICAL SOURCES

Sample Introductory Paragraph: Literary Analysis Research Essay Using Historical Sources

Davinder Lee's novel *Of Arrangements* is a complex text that dramatizes problems with the idea of love. To understand the significance of the relationship between the two protagonists and how their lives dramatize a commentary on love, it is important to know something about the culture in which the novel is set, that of New Zealand in the late 1970s. Considered in this context, the novel becomes not only a statement about the self-defeating attitude of individuals, but about society in general. *Of Arrangements* suggests that when a culture puts an illusory notion of love at its centre, it creates a world in which people can only see their own interest in the narrowest of terms, and this leads to self-destruction.

EXERCISE SET 5.4—UNDERSTANDING THE USE OF HISTORICAL SOURCES

Exercise 5.4 A (Answers are in Appendix 4)

1. What is the function of the historical sources cited in the first body paragraph of the literary analysis research essay using historical sources in Appendix 2 (page 117)?

2. What is the function of the historical sources cited in the second body paragraph of the essay referred to in question 1?

Exercise 5.4 B

1. Review a literary text you have been discussing in class. Establish where and when it was written and where and when it is set.

2. Name three important events that took place in the decade leading up to the first publication of the text, events of which the author would have been aware.

3. Develop three questions, relevant to issues in the literary text you are dealing with, that concern the ethos of the culture in which the story is set (such as the culture's religious beliefs, its attitude toward minorities, or its toleration of dissent).

4. Identify three details in the text you are working with that might appear more significant for your analysis if you researched them. (You could consider whether something a character eats is typical, whether a trip a character takes would have been easy or arduous, etc.)

Exercise 5.4 C

1. Take notes about the attitude of a character in the literary text you are analyzing to an important issue, whether a general one, such as individual freedom, or a more specific one, such as the right of women to vote.

2. Using historical sources, determine whether the character's attitude established in question 1 is typical of the time and culture in which the literary text is set.

3. Using the information you gathered in your answer to Exercise 5.4 B, question 4, write a short analytical paragraph about the significance of a detail in the literary text you are analyzing.

\\ IN-CLASS ESSAYS

In most English literature courses, you will be required to write one or more essays in class or as part of a final exam. You may be asked to write any of the types of essays described in this chapter. One common in-class assignment is to respond to a critic's comment about a text, stating whether you think the text is an example of the point the critic makes. Another common in-class assignment is the "sight poem," an essay on a poem that you have not read before. You may also be asked to write an essay on a poem that is one of a number that you have studied; you need to prepare for all of the poems, because you do not know ahead of time which will be chosen. Writing in-class essays can be difficult and stressful, but there are some simple techniques you can use to improve your results.

Gather as much information as you can about what you will be asked to do. Your instructor may be quite specific about the kind of essay you will be asked to write. Knowing whether you will be writing a comparative essay, a passage analysis essay, a sight poem essay, or some other kind of essay should make a difference in your preparation.

Even if you have carefully studied the literary texts you will be writing on during the term, go over them and take simple notes summarizing the texts. Most in-class essays, especially those given in final exams, do not allow students to consult the texts they are analyzing. The summaries will be useful as memory triggers to help you recall evidence. If, for example, you may be writing on a play, take notes on the main events of each act. In the exam, you are likely to be able to recall or even develop ideas about themes communicated by the play, but remembering specific evidence can be difficult. If you have a clear summary in your mind, whether covering the main events in a novel or play or the general content of each stanza in a short poem, you will more likely be able to recall specific details as needed. In the case of a sight poem, of course, you will have the text in front of you, so the difficulties will not be in recalling evidence. Give special attention to the resolution of conflicts in texts that have narrative structures, and, in poems, to crucial evidence that establishes the attitude toward the subject.

You should also write concise notes on the abstract topics raised by texts and the themes they express. Be prepared to be flexible. You might be asked to explain what a text suggests about a topic that you have not considered. You might be asked to compare two texts that you have not thought of in relation to each other.

The in-class essay puts pressure on the writing process. You will not have time to pre-write or to brainstorm very much, if at all. You can save time by relying on what you know about essay structure. You know what needs to be said in an introductory paragraph. You know how your analytical paragraphs need to begin. Do not panic over the details, such as whether you have repeated every key term in the correct order. Concentrate on fundamentals, such as making sure that you always analyze the evidence you present. When marking in-class work, instructors are generally less demanding about essay structure. You can be very confident, however, that clear paragraphs connecting claims to evidence and analysis will give your ideas the effective structure they deserve, and you will achieve much better results.

KEY POINTS

- Prepare for in-class essays by writing summaries of the texts you will need to analyze, in order to improve your recall of evidence.

- Pay particular attention to resolutions of conflicts, and to evidence in poems that establishes the attitude to the subject.

- Present your ideas in a well-structured essay.

The Modern Languages Association (MLA) format is standard in English literary studies. MLA gives instructions for the appearance of essays and explains how to acknowledge the sources used (documentation). This overview of MLA format is based on the *MLA Handbook for Writers of Research Papers* (7th ed.). More detailed information is available online at sites such as *Research and Documentation Online* and *The OWL at Purdue*, including information on other formats, such as American Psychological Association (APA).

\\ THE APPEARANCE OF THE ESSAY

A simple way to ensure that you present your work correctly is to use one of the essays in Appendix 2 as a guide. Follow the example for page numbering, margins, indenting of paragraphs, and the block of information that includes your name, your instructor's name, the course, and the date. A few points are worth emphasizing:

1. Do not enclose your essay in a cover or folder. Use a single staple or a paperclip.

2. Use standard white paper (not hole-punched).

3. Use a standard font such as Times New Roman or Times. Make the size 12-point. Do not put your title in bold, all-capitals, or a larger font.

4. Leave a single space after punctuation marks within sentences. After concluding punctuation marks, leave a single space, or two spaces if your instructor prefers that, but be consistent throughout.

5. Enclose within quotation marks the titles of stories, poems, essays, songs, short videos, and other short works. Italicize titles of books, journals, entire websites, feature films, and other longer works. (This instruction applies to titles of works within the title of your essay and within parenthetical references, as well as in the essay itself.)

6. Double-space throughout.

7. Do not use a separate title page unless your instructor asks you to do so.

8. Do not use contractions.

9. Capitalize each word in your title, except for prepositions, coordinating conjunctions, and articles, which are capitalized only if they begin a title or subtitle.

10. Ask your instructor if she or he requires any small changes in the format outlined here.

\\ DOCUMENTATION: WORKS CITED LIST

The Works Cited list appears on a separate page at the end of the essay. It includes every work to which you refer in the body of the essay. Do not include works that you have read but not referred to, even if they are related to your topic. Order the list alphabetically by author or by title if the author is unknown.

Many first- and second-year literary analysis essays have only one entry in the list of works cited. For examples of lists with several entries, see essays 7, 8, and 9 in Appendix 2. Note that the first line in each entry in the list begins flush with the left margin, and each subsequent line in the same entry is indented five spaces (half an inch) to the right. This "hanging indent" makes it easy to see where one entry ends and the next begins.

WORKS CITED ENTRIES: PRINT SOURCES

For books, give the author's name, then the title, publisher, and place and year of publication, concluding with an indication that the source is print. Add other details as needed, such as the name of a translator, an editor, an edition number, or the original date of publication. (See the sample entries below for the appropriate place to insert this information.)

For articles from periodicals, give the author's name, the title of the article, the title of the periodical, and publication information for the relevant periodical issue, including page numbers. End the entry with the medium of publication (e.g., print, web, etc.).

Sample Works Cited Entries for Print Sources

Book with One Author

> Highway, Tomson. *The Rez Sisters*. Saskatoon: Fifth House, 1988. Print.

Begin with the author's last name. Give a short version of the publisher's name, omitting generic words such as "Publishers," "Ltd.," "Co.," "Inc.," and "Press"; when the publisher is a university press, the abbreviation "UP" (with no periods) must be used.

Book with Two or Three Authors

> Brinton, Crane, John B. Christopher, and Robert Lee Wolff. *Modern Civilization: A History of the Last Five Centuries*. 2nd ed. Englewood Cliffs: Prentice-Hall, 1967. Print.

List the authors in the order they appear on the title page. Begin with the first author's last name. List subsequent authors in this entry with first name first.

Book with More Than Three Authors or Editors

> Guerin, Wilfred L., et al. *A Handbook of Critical Approaches to Literature*. 6th ed. New York: Oxford UP, 2010. Print.

Begin with the first of the authors listed on the title page. Use the Latin term "et al.," meaning "and others," to indicate that there are more authors. You may choose to list all the authors instead of using the abbreviation.

Work in an Anthology

Clarke, George Elliot. "Violets for Your Furs." 1994. *A New Anthology of Canadian Literature in English*. Ed. Donna Bennett and Russell Brown. Toronto: Oxford UP, 2002. 1153–54. Print.

Indicate the editor(s) after the anthology title; include the page numbers after the date of publication.

Several Works from One Anthology

Friedman, Elyse. "I Found Your Vox." Gartner 193–98.
Gartner, Zsuzsi, ed. *Darwin's Bastards: Astounding Tales from Tomorrow*. Toronto: Douglas and McIntyre, 2010. Print.
Malla, Pasha. "1999." Gartner 365–84.

Cross-reference by entering the entire anthology under the editor's name. List works from within the anthology by the author's last name, the title, the last name(s) of the anthology editor(s), and the page numbers.

Translation

Camus, Albert. "The Guest." Trans. Justin O'Brien. *The Story and Its Writer: An Introduction to Short Fiction*. 6th ed. Ed. Ann Charters. New York: Bedford, 2003. 211–20. Print.

Insert the abbreviation "Trans." and the name of the translator between the title of the translated story and the title of the book it's published in. (If O'Brien had translated the entire book, his name as translator would appear after the book's title.)

Article in a Scholarly Journal

Irish, Robert K. "'Let Me Tell You': About Desire and Narrativity in Graham Swift's *Waterland*." *Modern Fiction Studies* 44.4 (1998): 917–34. Print.

Indicate the volume and issue number after the journal title. Omit if the journal is not numbered.

Poem or Other Short Work in a Book by a Single Author

Lampman, Archibald. "June." *Lyrics of Earth*. Boston: Copeland and Day, 1895. 78–79. Print.

More Than One Work by an Author

> Fleming, Anne. *Anomaly*. Vancouver: Raincoast, 2005. Print.
> ---. *Pool-Hopping and Other Stories*. Victoria: Polestar, 1998. Print.

List the works alphabetically by title. For all entries after the first by the same author, substitute three hyphens for the author's name.

Book with No Known Author or Editor

> *Contemporary World Atlas*. New York: Rand McNally, 1986. Print.

List these works by their titles. Use a short version of the title in the parenthetical citation. For the example above, the short title would be *Contemporary* (in italics, since it's a book title).

Republished Book

> Novik, Mary. *Conceit*. 2007. Toronto: Anchor, 2008. Print.

Follow this format when a book is republished, not for a new edition.

Subsequent Edition

> Burroway, Janet, Elizabeth Stuckey-French, and Ned Stuckey-French. *Writing Fiction: A Guide to Narrative Craft*. 8th ed. New York: Pearson/Longman, 2011. Print.

Insert the number of the edition after the title.

Book Prepared by an Editor

> Fielding, Henry. *Tom Jones*. 1749. Ed. Sheridan Baker. New York: Norton, 1973. Print.

Insert the abbreviation "Ed." and the name(s) of the editor(s) after the original date of publication.

Article in a General Reference Book

> "Mutual Assured Destruction." *Canadian Oxford Dictionary*. 2nd ed. 2004. Print.

Where there is no author, start the entry with the title of the article; in a dictionary, this is the term whose definition you're citing. For widely used reference books, omit the publisher information. Also omit the page number and the volume if the articles are arranged alphabetically.

Article in a Specialized Reference Book

> Pennee, Donna Palmateer. "Flood, Cynthia." *The Oxford Companion to Canadian Literature*. 2nd ed. Toronto: Oxford UP, 1997. Print.

If the article has an author, the entry must begin with the author's name; if there is no author, begin with the title of the article. Here, "Flood, Cynthia" is the title of the article, not the author (hence the quotation marks). For specialized reference books, the publisher information is required. However, if the articles are arranged alphabetically then volume and page number can be omitted.

Introduction, Preface, Foreword, or Afterword

Manguel, Alberto. Introduction. *Going Ashore: Stories*. By Mavis Gallant. Toronto: McClelland and Stewart, 2009. xi–xiii. Print.

Begin with the name of the author of the specific part being cited, followed by the name of the part being cited.

Review

Wood, James. "Sons and Lovers." Rev. of *The Stranger's Child*, by Alan Hollinghurst. *The New Yorker* 17 Oct. 2011: 86. Print.

Include the title of the review if it has one, the abbreviation "Rev. of" for "Review of," and the title of the work being reviewed, followed by the publication information for the review.

Interview

Healey, Michael, and Layne Coleman. "The Writer Boy and the Director Boy." Interview by David Burgess. *Canadian Theatre Review* 108 (2001): 24–28. Print.

For the purposes of an interview, the author is considered to be the person being interviewed, not the interviewer. Give the appropriate publication information for the venue in which the interview appears—here, it is a journal article, but it may appear in a magazine or newspaper, in an anthology, online, or on television (see below for these formats).

WORKS CITED ENTRIES: ONLINE SOURCES

Following the author's name, give the title, publisher or sponsoring institution of the website (if unavailable, use the abbreviation "n.p."), the date the site was created or last revised (if unavailable, use "n.d."), an indication that the source is the web, and the date of access. MLA does not require URLs in citations. If your instructor asks you to add URLs, insert them in angle brackets (< >) after the date of access.

Sample Works Cited Entries for Online Sources

Article in an Online Scholarly Journal

Menze, Earnest A. "Johann Gottfried Herder and William James: Aspects of Anticipatory Thinking." *William James Studies* 7 (2011): 1–19. Web. 10 Nov. 2011.

If you find the article's full text in an online database, such as *EBSCO* or *Project Muse*, then you must also include the name of the database in italics, after the page numbers.

An Entire Website

> *Virginia Woolf Society of Great Britain*. The Virginia Woolf Society of Great Britain, n.d. Web. 12 Dec 2011.

The name of the website and the sponsoring institution are almost the same in this case.

An Article on a Website

> Clarke, S. N. "Virginia Woolf (1882–1941): A Short Biography." *Virginia Woolf Society of Great Britain*. The Virginia Woolf Society of Great Britain, 2000. Web. 12 Dec 2011.

If no author is given for the particular article being cited, then begin your entry with the title of the article.

Department Website

> *Department of English and Film Studies*. U of Alberta, n.d. Web. 4 May 2011.

Image

> Munch, Edvard. *The Scream*. 1893. The National Museum of Art, Architecture and Design, Oslo. *The National Museum of Art, Architecture and Design*. Web. 24 May 2011.

List by the artist's name. Give the title of the work, the date of creation, if available, the institution that holds the work, and the city. The name of the website may be similar to the name of the institution.

Works Cited Entries: Other Non-Print Sources

Audio Recording

> Mitchell, Joni. "The Fiddle and the Drum." *Clouds*. Reprise, 1969. LP.

Include the name of the record label before the date.

Film

> *Dr. Strangelove or: How I Learned to Stop Worrying and Love the Bomb*. Dir. Stanley Kubrick. Columbia Pictures, 1964. Film.

If relevant, list performer names after the director's name. Use the abbreviation "Perf.," meaning "performed by," to head the list. If your source is a DVD, substitute the distributor's name for the studio's and replace "Film" with "DVD." If you viewed the film by streaming video online, give the name of the service or website (in italics) followed by the information for an online source: e.g., *NFB-ONF*. Web. 30 Apr. 2012.

Television Program

> "Betty and Veronica." *Veronica Mars*. CBS. KIRO, Seattle, 29 Mar. 2005. Television.

List the title of the episode, the name of the program or series, the network name, call letters of the broadcasting station followed by the city, and the date of broadcast.

Recorded Television Program

> "Betty and Veronica." *Veronica Mars: The Complete First Season*. Warner Home Video, 2005. DVD.

Instead of broadcasting details, provide the distributor name, the date of distribution, and the publication medium.

\\ DOCUMENTATION: IN-TEXT CITATIONS

In the body of your essay, the phrases with which you introduce a quotation or paraphrase, such as "according to ... " or " ... states," provide some information about the source. A parenthetical citation following the quotation or paraphrase gives additional information.

For most print sources and for electronic sources in which page numbers are given, parenthetical citations usually include the page number(s) of the passage cited. For poetry, use the word "line" or "lines," followed by the line numbers of the passage cited, the *first* time you cite the work; thereafter, give only the numbers themselves. For electronic sources in which page numbers are not given, use the abbreviation "par(s)." for "paragraphs," followed by the paragraph number.

Avoid repeating information in your parenthetical citations that you have already provided. Whether more information is needed in the parenthetical citation, such as the author's name, depends on what information is given in the surrounding text of the essay.

Sample Parenthetical Citations

The Author Is Named in The Sentence

> Dickstein describes how "the mania of national security ... ruined the lives of some [and] touched many others with the cold hand of fear and conformity" (26–27).

Include only the page number within the parenthetical citation.

The Author of The Literary Work Is Clear

> The narrator of "The Guest" says that Daru "lives like a Monk" (212).

The introductory phrase does not mention the author directly, but the reader knows that the topic of the essay is Albert Camus's story "The Guest." The narrator is a figure from that story, so the name "Camus" does not need to appear in the citation. When you quote or paraphrase a literary text in this manner, the reader will usually know the author of the work because you have stated it earlier in the essay.

The Author's Name Is Not Given in the Sentence

> It has been argued that some historians "simplify, finalize, and even brutally exclude" (Decoste 390).

Include the author's name in the parenthetical citation so that the reader can find the work, listed alphabetically by author, in the list of works cited.

The Author's Name Is Not Given, and the Essay Cites More than One Work by That Author

> It has been argued that some historians "simplify, finalize, and even brutally exclude" (Decoste, *Question* 390).

Include a short version of the title of the work in the parenthetical citation, distinguishing it from other works by the same author in the list of works cited.

The Quotation or Paraphrase Is from a Sacred Text

> Jesus said, "Love your enemies" (The Bible, King James Version, Matt. 5.44).

Indicate which version of the sacred text you are using, followed by the names or numbers of the relevant sections, such as book, chapter, and verse of the Bible. In following parenthetical references, only book, chapter, and verse are required.

Always ask yourself whether there is enough information in your sentence and the parenthetical citation for the reader to be able to find the relevant work in the list of works cited. Review the essays in Appendix 2 to see more examples of how in-text citations are presented.

\\ FORMATTING QUOTATIONS

SHORT QUOTATIONS

Quotations of no more than four lines of prose (in your essay, not the original text) or four lines of poetry should be enclosed within double quotation marks and integrated into the text. A parenthetical citation follows the quotation, usually including a page, line, or paragraph number.

Sample Short Quotations

Short Quotation with Added Punctuation

> Slocum confesses, "I get the willies when I see closed doors," and he adds, "Something must have happened to me sometime" (5).

The comma after "doors" does not appear in the original (*Something Happened*, by Joseph Heller). It is added, within the quotation marks, to make the sentence correct. The original has a period after "sometime." In the quotation, the period is placed after the parenthetical citation, outside the quotation marks. (This change in the final punctuation is one of the *very few* permissible changes to a quotation.)

Short Quotation Ending in a Question Mark or Exclamation Mark

> Slocum asks, "Will I have to endure and survive these same assaults and rejections from my little boy when he grows up too?" (193).

Place a question mark or exclamation mark within the quotation marks if it is part of the quoted passage. Add a period after the parenthetical citation, if the quotation ends the sentence.

Short Poetry Quotation with Line Breaks

> The speaker of Karen Houle's "During, Three" observes, "I stand like soldier's doubt / at the lake" (3–4).

A slash, with a space before and after, indicates the line break.

LONG QUOTATIONS

Set off quotations of four lines or more of prose or poetry by starting the quotation on a new line and indenting one inch from the left margin. (Do not indent the right margin.)

Sample Long Quotations

Long Prose Quotation

> Slocum describes his son's problems:

> My little boy is having a difficult time of it in school this year, in gym, in math, and in classes stressing public speaking. And just about everywhere else, it seems. (At home with me. With my wife. My daughter. My boy seems to be having a difficult time of it in school every year now when the new term starts, but each year seems to grow worse. He is, I'm afraid, starting to "let me down.") (217)

Double-space the quotation. Do not use quotation marks unless a quotation occurs within the passage. The parenthetical citation follows any end punctuation.

Long Poetry Quotation

In Karen Houle's "During, Three," the speaker's description of the lakeside connects the natural world to a complicated sense of time:

> The former and genuine forever
> stretches out on all sides.
>
> Granite greyed face
> streaked salt pink. (8–11)

Maintain original line breaks, and keep the appearance as close to the original as you can. Notice that the parenthetical reference is giving line numbers, not page numbers, for poetry.

CHANGING QUOTATIONS

Sometimes it is necessary to change quotations in order to integrate them grammatically with your sentences or other quotations, or to make meaning clear. Present quotations in such a way as to keep changes to a minimum. Examples in this section are based on the following passage from *Rainforest Narratives: The Work of Janette Turner Hospital*, by David Callahan:

> The principal male figure who might counter the powerful pull of the absent father is ironically also absent—Mishka's Uncle Otto, whose image appears to Mishka at moments of great stress, as if calling him back to the positive realities associated with his mother's side of the family, and above all to the realities of music. (288)

Quotation with Word(s) Added

Callahan observes that Uncle Otto's image seems to be "calling him [Mishka] back to the positive realities associated with his mother's side of the family, and above all to the realities of music" (288).

Enclose the added words within square brackets to indicate that they do not appear in the original. The addition is needed because without it "him" would be unclear.

Quotation with Word(s) Deleted

Callahan notes that "The principal male figure who might counter the powerful pull of the absent father is . . . Mishka's Uncle Otto" (288).

Use ellipsis (three spaced periods) to indicate that words have been omitted. The words are omitted from the quotation because the writer wants to focus only on part of Callahan's point. The remaining sentence must be logically and grammatically complete, and it must be faithful to the original author's meaning.

Poetry Quotation with A Line or More Omitted

The speaker of Houle's "During, Three" describes a series of features of the landscape:

Granite greyed face
streaked salt pink.

Jack pines penetrated
by sturdy bugs.

Stunned cones, cached.
Skirt caves of spruce.

. . . .
A fogged rock rounded back. (10–18)

Indicate the omitted lines with a series of spaced periods of roughly the same length as a line from the poem. Two lines are omitted from the example above because they do not describe features of the landscape that the writer wants to analyze.

SAMPLE ESSAYS

The following literary analysis essays apply the method described in this book. All of the essays are useful as examples. Go through them to identify the key elements: the thesis and the analytical claims. Read the thesis and claims over to see if they form a logical argument. Go over the body paragraphs carefully, noting the key words in the claims and in the analyses. Review the introductory paragraphs and make note of the key elements. Make notes about how the essays could be improved. Note that the Works Cited lists are included with the last page of each essay, in order to save space in this text; unless your instructor specifically asks you to do otherwise, present your Works Cited list on a separate page.

The following is a brief description of each essay, in the order in which they appear. Very successful students wrote these essays. Their level of study is indicated in parentheses after the description.

1. "Freedom and Attachment in 'The Guest,' by Albert Camus" analyzes a short story. (2nd year)

2. "Unnatural Humanity: An Analysis of Wallace Stevens's 'Anecdote of the Jar'" analyzes a poem (which is provided before the essay). The essay includes a consideration of some of the poem's formal features. (2nd year)

3. "Dreams, Family, and Love in Tomson Highway's *The Rez Sisters*" analyzes a play. (1st year)

4. "Individualism in *The Way of All Flesh*" analyzes a novel. (2nd year)

5. "The Visual Characterization of Power in *Dr. Strangelove*" analyzes a film. (1st year)

6. "The Power of the Minority: An Analysis of Louise Erdrich's 'Scales'" analyzes a short story. It focuses on a single passage from the story and shows how the passage contributes to the story's theme. (1st year)

7. "Two Views of Sexual Desire in 'The Cinnamon Peeler' and 'Violets for Your Furs'" is a comparative essay that analyzes two poems. (2nd year)

8. "Suspicious History: About the Ending of Graham Swift's *Waterland*" uses critical sources to support an analysis of a novel. (4th year)

9. "Conformity and Evil in John Cheever's 'The Five-Forty-Eight'" uses historical sources to support an analysis of a short story. (2nd year)

\\ 1. A LITERARY ANALYSIS ESSAY ON A SHORT STORY

Julia Chen

Dr. Paul Headrick

ENGL 1127

September 12, 2006

Freedom and Attachment in
"The Guest," by Albert Camus

Albert Camus's philosophically complex story "The Guest" is about individual freedom and personal attachments. Through the main character's geographic circumstances, his relationship with the prisoner, and the resolution of the story's central conflicts, the story makes an important commentary on the limitations of freedom. Ultimately, "The Guest" insists that although individuals might conceive of themselves as free, they are inescapably connected to the people around them and must accept and foster these attachments.

Daru's physical surroundings create an impression of unlimited freedom and detachment. The narrator describes the land surrounding Daru's schoolhouse, where he "lives like a monk" (212), as a "high, deserted plateau" (211) and as a "solitary expanse where nothing had any connection with man" (213). The altitude suggested by the term "high" and the wide open space suggested by "deserted plateau" and "solitary expanse" evoke an absence of obstacles and a freedom to do whatever one wants. The description of the landscape as having no "connection with man" implies an existence that is detached from human concerns, as does the fact that Daru lives in isolation, "like a monk." The descriptions imply that freedom and detachment are linked.

In his relationship with the Arab prisoner, Daru experiences a conflict between individual freedom and attachment to another. As the story's ironic title suggests, Daru treats the man not as a prisoner but as a "guest": he feeds him, offers him a bed, and sleeps near him unarmed. His hospitality implies that Daru feels responsible for the man's well-being. Yet when the man asks, "Why do you eat with me?" Daru replies, "I'm hungry" (216). Daru's response suggests that despite his feeling of responsibility, he resists the idea of a relationship with the man. Rather than offering an explanation that has something to do with the man, Daru focuses on himself and his own hunger. The tension between freedom and attachment is also evident when Daru sends the prisoner off with food, money, and directions to both the police station and the shelter of the nomads. By providing the man with basic necessities, Daru implicitly acknowledges his attachment to him. His refusal to advise the man, however, suggests a desire to remain free from attachments or responsibilities to another.

Through both the prisoner's decision to turn himself in and his family's threat to Daru, the story suggests that personal attachments are powerful and inescapable. Before Daru and the prisoner go to sleep, the prisoner asks Daru if he will be accompanying him to Tinguit. When Daru says he doesn't know, the man says, "Come with us" (217). The urgency of his request, phrased as an invitation or a command, suggests that he feels an attachment to Daru. The power of this attachment is evident when, after being left to do as he pleases, the man expresses "a sort of panic" then stands "looking at the schoolmaster" with "his arms hanging" (219) before taking the road to prison. The man's "panic" suggests that complete freedom distresses him, while his "hanging" arms imply an inability to act on his freedom. By looking at Daru then taking the road to prison, the man suggests that his attachment to the schoolmaster guides his actions more powerfully than does his free will. The power of personal attachments is also, of course, emphasized through the message written on Daru's chalkboard: "You handed over our brother. You will pay for this" (220). Although Daru has tried to detach himself from other people, the message on the board, particularly the reference to communal brotherhood, clearly suggests that such detachment is impossible. The remark that Daru must "pay for this" further implies, metaphorically, that the consequences of his attachments to other people are inescapable.

The story's resolution implies that the freedom connected to isolation is illusory, and our attachments to other people must be accepted and even fostered. After Daru returns to the schoolhouse and discovers the message left for him, the narrator says that he "looked at the sky, the plateau, and, beyond, the invisible lands stretching all the way to the sea" and that in this "vast landscape he had loved so much, he was alone" (220). These final references to the "vast," -unobstructed surroundings of sky, plateau, and lands that stretch far away evoke once again the idea of freedom. Yet the evocations of freedom are ironic, for Daru is not free. His inescapable connection to the Arab prisoner has cost him his life, and his love of freedom and autonomy, suggested here by his love for the "vast landscape," has left him merely "alone," without protection. The narrator's use of the past perfect tense in the phrase "he had loved" implies that Daru's commitment to freedom has been shaken and that he realizes on some level that he would have been better off with closer attachments to other people.

Ultimately, "The Guest" challenges the modern ideal of individual freedom. Through its bleak ending, it reminds us that detaching ourselves from relationships with others is not only impossible but also dangerous. A further study might analyze the story in the context of the French colonial experience in Algeria and consider how its comment on individuals could be applied to global politics.

Work Cited

Camus, Albert. "The Guest." Translated by Justin O'Brien. *The Story and Its Writer: An Introduction to Short Fiction*, edited by Ann Charters, 6th ed., Bedford/St. Martin's, 2003, pp. 211–20.

\\ 2. A LITERARY ANALYSIS ESSAY ON A POEM

ANECDOTE OF THE JAR

I placed a jar in Tennessee,
And round it was, upon a hill.
It made the slovenly wilderness
Surround that hill.

The wilderness rose up to it,
And sprawled around, no longer wild.
The jar was round upon the ground
And tall and of a port in air.

It took dominion everywhere.
The jar was gray and bare.
It did not give of bird or bush,
Like nothing else in Tennessee.

Wallace Stevens
From *The Collected Poems of Wallace Stevens*, by Vintage.

Jeff Brin

Dr. Paul Headrick

English 1129

3 November 2003

Unnatural Humanity: An Analysis of Wallace Stevens's

"Anecdote of the Jar"

Wallace Stevens's short poem "Anecdote of the Jar" is about the relationship between humanity and nature. Through its central symbol, the poem establishes an opposition between humans and the natural world. Subtly, it criticizes humanity for its destructive domination of the natural world.

Initially, the poem suggests that even a slight human intrusion into the natural world is powerful and positive. The "jar" is the focus of attention of the title and of the poem itself. It is the only human-made thing referred to in the poem. This emphasis on the jar suggests it is a symbol. Its uniqueness as a thing made by people implies that it represents human creation. In the first quatrain, the speaker describes the wilderness into which he places the jar as "slovenly" (line 3). The jar, however, acts on the wilderness, so that it makes the wilderness "[s]urround" (4) the hill on which the jar is placed; the wilderness then is "no longer wild" (6). The word "slovenly" suggests a negative, untidy quality to the wilderness. The word "surrounds" suggests that the wilderness is controlled and drawn in by the jar and what it represents. The jar, moreover, clearly transforms nature, for if the wilderness is no longer wild, it is also not simply no longer slovenly; it is no longer a wilderness. Symbolically, then, the poem suggests that the intrusion of even a single, small human creation positively transforms nature.

An internal rhyme emphasizes the idea of the power of human creation. In the first and second quatrains the speaker describes the jar as "round" (2, 7), which rhymes internally with "Surround" (4) in the first stanza and "around" (6) and "ground" (6) in the second. The repetition of "round" stresses the human-made quality of the jar, for its roundness is not produced by nature. The connection the rhyme makes between a quality in the jar and the changed quality of the wilderness reinforces the idea that the wilderness is conforming to the roundness of the jar. Though the wilderness is as vast as an entire state, and the human creation is only an insignificant jar, the human creation exerts power over the wilderness.

The poem shifts in the final quatrain, expressing the idea that the effect of human creation on nature is ultimately destructive. The speaker says that the jar "takes dominion" (8) and describes the jar as "gray and bare" (10). The jar is then contrasted with all of Tennessee, as being the only thing that does not "give of bird or bush" (11). To "take dominion" is

The first citation to a line of poetry should include the word "line," specifying that the number given is that of a line in a poem. Subsequent citations include only the number.

The square brackets indicate that a change has been made to the original quoted material. In this case, the original is a capital "S." Keep such changes to a minimum.

to dominate, and "gray" and "bare" connote lifelessness and suggest that human creation, and the nature affected by it, will be lifeless. The poem suggests that the dominating jar will spread its lifelessness to nature. The effect of the final line, which contrasts the jar's lifelessness with everything else, is even stronger, as it makes clear that all of nature is productive, but human creation is not. The poem in this way criticizes human intrusions into nature for their dominating and destructively infertile effects.

The initially positive view of the human creation that the poem presents, then, is ironic. The poem suggests that seeing nature's apparent chaos as "slovenly" is an imposition of a false human value; in fact, nature is more full of positive life than the unproductive and uncreative thing that humans make of it as soon as they encounter it.

Work Cited

Stevens, Wallace. "Anecdote of the Jar." 1923. *The Norton Anthology of American Literature*, edited by Nina Baym, shorter 6th ed., Norton, 2003, p. 1926.

\\ 3. A LITERARY ANALYSIS ESSAY ON A PLAY*

Michael Ages
Dr. Paul Headrick
English 1129
June 28, 2006

Dreams, Family, and Love in
Tomson Highway's *The Rez Sisters*

Tomson Highway's play *The Rez Sisters* is about dreams, family, and love. The characters in the play are subtly connected through a symbolic pattern. These connections and the strange appearances by the mystical character Nanabush are crucial to one of the play's central themes. The play suggests that a certain kind of modern dream blinds us to the important things in life that are within reach: love and family.

The women on the reserve have dreams that suggest they sense that a satisfactory life in their community is impossible, and that they are incapable of changing their lives on their own. Soon after learning about the

---

*Reproduced with permission of Michael Ages.

Biggest Bingo in the World, Annie, Marie-Adele, and Veronique each, in turn, describe their dreams. Each of the women begins by saying "when I win the Biggest Bingo in the World" (35–36). Annie describes being able to "go to every record store [and] all the night clubs in Toronto" (35). Marie-Adele describes being able to buy an island. Veronique describes travelling to Paris and becoming a "rich and famous" (37) chef. All of the women's dreams involve moving to other places. The dreams show that the women feel that what they desire cannot be attained in their community, and that they imagine separating themselves from the community. The fact that the women imagine achieving their dreams after winning the Biggest Bingo shows that they feel that they need some outside force if they are to improve their lives; they feel they are incapable of achieving their dreams through their own efforts.

The community is portrayed positively, however, through Marie-Adele. The other women revere her home and children. Veronique says, of Marie-Adele's children, "Imagine. And all from one father" (21). Her comment is a joke that makes fun of the instability of family on the reserve, but it also expresses sincere admiration. The "14-post white picket fence" (18) in Marie-Adele's yard is mentioned several times. The white picket fence is an obvious symbol of a stable, traditional home, and the numerous references to it call attention to it and suggest it is a symbol of home. The fence's location at Marie-Adele's house reinforces the image of Marie-Adele's home-life as positive and stable.

The importance of community in the play is hinted at by a subtle symbolic pattern that connects the characters to Marie-Adele. At the beginning of Annie's description of her dreams concerning the Biggest Bingo, she says that her lucky bingo number is B14. Directly after Annie, Marie-Adele, and Veronique have described their dreams, Zhaboonigan runs after them and counts to fourteen. There are, as has been mentioned, fourteen fence posts. Most importantly, Marie-Adele has fourteen children. Annie's lucky number does not come up at the bingo game. The correspondence between the bingo number and the number of Marie-Adele's children ironically suggests that real good fortune is connected to family, not bingo and what it represents. Zhaboonigan's ability to count to fourteen hints that what she is capable of is tied to her membership in the family. The connection between the number of fence posts and the number of children implies that the fence is not simply a clichéd representation of a middle-class family, but is specifically connected to Marie-Adele and her children. The repeated references to the fence imply the importance placed on the children. Together, these connections imply that what is truly positive in their lives is, in fact, in their community: family and home.

The events at the bingo game, particularly Marie-Adele's experience, reinforce the idea of the importance of home and community. In her encounter with Nanabush the night before the Biggest Bingo, Marie-Adele, after realizing that Nanabush intends to take her life, says, "Not yet. Give me time. Please. Don't" (92). Her plea clearly shows that she is not ready to die. She still dreams of winning the bingo game and moving to an island. In describing the bingo to be played for the Biggest Bingo in the World, Nanabush, as the Bingo Master, says, "full house, ladies and gentlemen, full house" (102), which refers to the number of participants and also to filling one's entire bingo card to win the game. But the phrase also suggests Marie-Adele's house, which, with fourteen children, is certainly full. At the end of the game the Bingo Master whispers to Marie-Adele, "Bingo" (103). Since she has not won the bingo game in the most obvious sense, what is suggested is that she has won in another sense, through her actual full house. When Nanabush comes again to take her life, Marie-Adele says, "come ... beautiful ... dark wings ... take me" (104). The complete reversal in Marie-Adele's attitude to her impending death suggests that she now recognizes that she has already won the prize, through her family and her place in the community; she is satisfied with her life and able to face its end.

The fate of the other characters in the resolution of the play suggests that the modern ideal represented by the dreams the characters describe needs to be revised, in order to incorporate community and family. After Marie-Adele's death, Veronique assumes the role of homemaker in the Starblanket home. The stage notes describe her as "glowing with happiness" (110). Annie says, of her feelings for her bandmate Fritz the Katz, "I love him" (108). The description of Veronique shows emphatically that she is very satisfied with the way things have turned out for her. She is cooking, not to gain fame, but to feed a family in her community. Annie's acknowledgment of her feelings for Fritz suggests that music will find its place in her life through her relationship, not outside of it. Both Veronique and Annie have achieved good portions of the dreams they described earlier in the play. Their success shows that they were wrong to think that their dreams were unattainable without the help of bingo and the selfishness, even greed, that it represents. Their rebellion at the bingo game shows that they have repudiated their selfishness and the culture that lured them away from their community. Nanabush's final appearance shows that the ending is a positive one. In the foreword, Nanabush is described as being as "important a figure in the Native world as Christ is in Christian Mythology" (xii). Just before the play ends, Nanabush appears one last time and dances "merrily and triumphantly" (118). The dance shows that Nanabush is pleased with the way things have turned out for the women, and his opinion is clearly one that the play establishes as authoritative.

The Rez Sisters asserts the importance and power of love and family in the most difficult cultural circumstances. This essay has not considered the way in which the play also dramatizes issues between women and men on the reserve. A further study could consider this evidence and the way the play comments on gender relations and their significance in a community struggling to stay intact.

Work Cited

Highway, Tomson. *The Rez Sisters*. Fifth House, 1988.

\\ 4. A LITERARY ANALYSIS ESSAY ON A NOVEL*

Dani Lau
Dr. Paul Headrick
English 2224
3 Nov 2011

Individualism in Samuel Butler's
The Way of All Flesh

The Way of All Flesh can be read as a study of individualism. The protagonist, Ernest, evolves from living a passive, prescribed life to breaking out and living an active (though at times clumsy), independent life. Through the position Ernest reaches at the end of the novel and the way he contrasts with his parents, the novel criticizes passive acceptance of religion, tradition, and male authority, and celebrates a questioning individualism.

Through Theobald, Ernest's father, the novel presents traditional religious life as passive. The narrator, Overton, notes that "It had never so much as crossed Theobald's mind to doubt the literal accuracy of any syllable in the Bible" (81). Theobald's complete lack of doubt suggests that he does not choose between doubt and faith—he passively accepts his religion rather than choosing it. Theobald's passivity is not, however, unusual. Overton notes that "[i]n those days people believed with a simple downrightness which I do not observe among educated men and women now" (81). Overton contrasts a traditional "those days," negatively associated with passivity in religion, with a more modern, active, educated present. His comments connect religion with ignorance and imply a criticism of the unquestioning, passive acceptance of religion represented by Theobald.

* Reproduced with permission of Danielle Lau.

The novel's critical attitude to Theobald's passive religiosity is made clear in the one moment when he demonstrates a potential to be a more authentic individual. Early in his life Theobald asserts that he does not want to become ordained. Theobald's father responds with a threat: "You shall not receive a single sixpence from me till you come to your senses" (66). Overton states that "[e]ither Theobald's heart failed him, or he interpreted the outward shove which his father gave him as the inward call for which I have no doubt he prayed with great earnestness—for he was a firm believer in the efficacy of prayer" (66). The dramatic irony is clear. Theobald's resistance to ordination is an expression of an inner, authentic self, but the threat frightens Theobald into accepting his father's will. Theobald interprets his response to this "shove" from his father as evidence of his true spiritual calling. Theobald's passive acceptance of religion and the male authority represented by his father is self-serving rather than truly spiritual, and in this way the novel criticizes passive acceptance of what is given.

Through Theobald's relationship with Christina, Ernest's mother, the text extends its criticism of religion to include male authority. After they marry, Theobald takes complete control over Christina. He fantasizes about divorcing her over a trivial issue: her resistance to ordering dinner. Her capitulation to his authority is complete: "Dearest Theobald—dearest Theobald, forgive me; I have been very, very wrong" (88). Overton says that Christina becomes the "most devotedly obsequious wife in all of England" (89) and her "principle duty was, as she well said, to her husband—to love him, honour him, and keep him in good temper" (99). The way in which Christina pleads for forgiveness suggests that she regards her husband as if he is a priest, with a special authority just because he is a man, and that she thinks of her disagreement with him, however slight, as a serious sin. Theobald and Christina together make the idea that men are natural authorities look ridiculous.

Ernest, in contrast with his parents, represents individual questioning of traditional religion, including male authority. As a child, Ernest is unhappy with the way he is supposed to live. Overton describes the way he internalizes his parents' values and questions them at the same time:

> He hated Papa, and did not like Mamma, and this was what none but a bad and ungrateful boy would do after all that had been done for him. Besides, he did not like Sunday; he did not like anything that was really good; his tastes were low and such as he was ashamed of. He liked people best if they sometimes swore a little, so long as it was not at him. (152)

Ernest's hatred for his father clearly suggests his hatred for male authority and for unthinking acceptance of religion. Ernest does "not like" his mother, who also represents passive religion. She is less responsible, however, because she has given authority over to her husband, so Ernest does not go so far as to "hate" her. Ernest's response to the Sabbath emphasizes the connection between his opposition to his parents and to his questioning of religion itself. The Sabbath becomes part of a list of the things for which Ernest has negative feelings, and each item on the list is connected to the others. The shame that Ernest feels and his sense that he is bad show the power of the cultural forces his parents represent, and the way he has internalized his parents' values. The persistence of his hatred and his dislike shows his deep impulse to question those forces despite their power. His positive feelings for those who swear, demonstrating their resistance to religion, shows again that he cannot bring himself to passively accept the traditional religion that his parents represent.

The source of Ernest's questioning of traditional religion and male authority is his authentic, individual self. Overton observes that Ernest had been taught that "pleasure had in it something more or less sinful" (157). Later, Overton describes Ernest's feelings as he works on his organ: "Ernest's sallow face was flushed with his work, and his eyes were sparkling with pleasure . . . . His inner self never told him that this was humbug, as it did about Latin or Greek" (173–74). The text clearly suggests that the pleasure Ernest feels is positive. The key term in the passage is "inner self." Following the dictates of this inner self is the source of the pleasure, and since the pleasure is valued, so is the source of the value, the inner, authentic self, operating autonomously rather than according to the dictates of religion. Accepting the value of his pleasure means that Ernest rejects what he has been taught. The study of Latin and Greek is a traditional part of Victorian education. Ernest's feeling that it is "humbug," is another sign of his questioning of tradition and the strength of his individual self.

Through Ernest's eventual success, *The Way of All Flesh* expresses its approval of individualism. Ernest finally achieves independence from his parents, especially his father, and he is a financial success. Overton quotes Ernest's publisher, describing Ernest: "'He is in a very solitary position . . . . He has formed no alliances, and has made enemies not only of the religious world but of the literary and scientific brotherhood as well. This will not do nowadays'" (429). This complaint about Ernest's individualism ironically emphasizes the novel's approval of that very quality. It shows that Ernest's intellectual independence and autonomy are deep. He is not only financially independent, but he is able to discard the conventions of his religious tradition and move toward true individualism.

Through the clear contrast between Ernest and his parents, and the way in which Ernest develops, *The Way of All Flesh* presents something like a secular sermon, preaching against the evils of a traditional religion that prescribes passivity, gives too much authority to men, and denies individualism. This essay has not considered the way in which the novel's valuing of progress and individual reason could also be considered Victorian.

Work Cited

Butler, Samuel. *The Way of All Flesh*. 1903. Edited by James Cochrane, Penguin, 1986.

\\ 5. A LITERARY ANALYSIS ESSAY ON A FILM*

Chris Shalom
Dr. Peter Babiak
ENGL 1130
Nov. 10, 2011

The Visual Characterization of Power in *Dr. Strangelove*

Stanley Kubrick's satirical film *Dr. Strangelove* is about our attitude to violence and power. The military leaders are among the chief targets of the satire, but though the film makes these leaders ridiculous, the cinematography suggests that they have significantly more power and freedom than the other characters in the film. The way the leaders are shot, however, especially the camera angles used, contributes to the film's argument that those who command the power of violence do not deserve the admiration conventionally granted them.

In an early military base scene, the camera angles contribute to a characterization of General Ripper as powerful, especially in relation to Captain Mandrake. As Ripper reveals to Mandrake his plan to cause nuclear war, he is shot in an extremely low-angle close-up. A low angle establishes power for the featured subject, with the amount of power increasing relative to the degree of the angle. General Ripper's rank makes him more powerful than Mandrake, and the camera angle emphasizes this power. In the same scene, Mandrake's coverage is a medium, low-angle close-up, but the angle is significantly less extreme than Ripper's coverage. While the coverage of Mandrake uses similar compositional techniques—a close-up and a low angle—it reduces the extremity of both these power-associated elements, and thereby reduces the suggestion of power.

* Reproduced with permission of Chris Shalom.

In the war room, General Turgidson is similarly shot in contrast to President Muffley to signify power for Turgidson and subordination for Muffley. Turgidson is framed in a diagonal composition with strong leading lines created by the generals seated at the war-room table. The other generals are in soft focus. The diagonal composition leading to Turgidson suggests his dominance over the rest of the military leaders. The soft focus makes the other generals indistinguishable, evoking the idea of a faceless mob and suggesting their individual lack of power. President Muffley, in contrast with Turgidson, is shot roughly at eye level and is placed in a much denser and more muddled frame. The angle gives him no power, and the composition draws focus away from him and makes him less dominant. Unlike the diagonal composition of Turgidson's coverage, Muffley's frame is a circular composition. The circular shot does not direct attention to Muffley and so suggests his limited power.

At the same time that the cinematography emphasizes the power of Ripper and Turgidson, it hints at the conventionally admiring attitude society has toward such figures. The view of Ripper, who is seen from below with jutting cigar and many military decorations, lit from above and isolated in the frame by a black background, evokes the view from the bottom of a massive military statue. This viewpoint suggests he is worthy of permanent public display, someone to be admired and idolized. In the war-room scenes, the faceless generals have a similar appearance to Turgidson, wearing similar clothing and striking similar postures. The composition thus imbues Turgidson with greater power than he would have as a single character, as he appears both to represent and to command a large, admiring group.

The cinematography in the bomber scenes and during the military base firefight conveys the unimportance of those who commit violence without really having power. In contrast to the highly controlled, formalist approach to cinematography in the war-room and interior military base scenes, the bomber flight crew and the American soldiers outside the military base are shot with a largely realist approach. The angles are wide, and the realist technique evokes newsreel war footage. The newsreel feel suggests the unimportance of the individuals. In the military base firefight sequence, for example, the soldiers are shown mostly in extreme wide shots, which, in combination with the shaky handheld camera, make it difficult to distinguish any one individual from the other soldiers. In the bomber, the crew members are placed in highly dense frames, often with significant foreground and background subjects that draw attention away from them. These techniques, again, reduce the visual impact of individual characters, making them appear unimportant and diminishing any impression of their power. Especially in contrast to the close-ups of Ripper and the dominant imagery of Turgidson, the cinematography in these scenes emphasizes the wide gap in power between the generals and the soldiers.

The cinematography further accentuates the gap in freedom and power between the military officials and the lower-ranked soldiers through its differing approaches to the use of space. Throughout the film, scenes in the war room are shot with open forms, allowing characters to move freely within the frame. This ability to move, especially when considered in contrast with closed frame compositions in the bomber, suggests more freedom for the generals and high-ranking politicians in the war room. The characters in the war room are often covered by tracking dolly shots when they are in motion. Instead of being contained by a static perspective, the tracking shots make the characters in the war room appear free to move throughout the larger environment. The ability of the characters to move outside the initial frame, and even to guide the camera's shift in perspective, suggests their greater freedom and power. In contrast, the bomber crew members move in and out of frames without any apparent impact on the camera's perspective. Rather than the characters being free to move and remain dominant in frames, it is the camera which has the ability to move freely in these scenes. The way in which the crew members are constrained visually suggests their limited power.

The resolution of the film emphatically dramatizes a condemnation of the powerful and violent and the danger of admiring them. The attack launched by the powerful and insane General Ripper leads to the world's destruction. Through his responsibility for bringing about doomsday, the film links violent military power with a kind of perverse insanity and condemns it. The leaders in the war room are responsible for putting in place the weapons systems that destroy the world, and they too are helpless to stop the destruction. In the final interior shots of the bomber, though there are brief close-ups of different members of the flight crew, the camera spends as much time on the control panels as the plane approaches the target. The shots cut quickly from the men to the controls. The close-ups of the controls and the quick cuts suggest a kind of unthinking obedience on the part of the crew. They act in the service of the technology and give up their wills to do the will of their superiors, contributing to the end of the world. The film suggests that the powerful are, to say the least, unworthy of our admiration, for their power is linked to a kind of evil insanity. The cinematography satirizes the way in which such figures are conventionally glorified and admired.

The cinematography in *Dr. Strangelove* emphasizes the power of certain characters and contributes to the satire that attacks military authority and our admiration for it. This essay has not considered the way in which the film's satirical attack gains force when considered in its cold war context. A further study could consider that context, and the way in which the power that is satirized is connected to a debased idea of masculinity.

Work Cited

Dr. Strangelove or: How I Learned to Stop Worrying and Love the Bomb.
Directed by Stanley Kubrick, Columbia Pictures, 1964.

\\ 6. A PASSAGE ANALYSIS ESSAY*

David Mongar
Dr. Paul Headrick
English 1127
November 20, 2007

The Power of the Minority: An Analysis of Louise Erdrich's "Scales"

"Scales," by Louise Erdrich, is a story about inequality and change. In a key passage in the story, Gerry enters the weighshack and is reunited with Dot. The passage is crucial because it reveals Gerry's power, his magical qualities, and his peaceful nature, and it elevates him to an extraordinary status while demonstrating the purity of the love he shares with Dot. In the resolution these qualities are distilled into Dot and Gerry's child, expressing the story's theme, which is that even if a minority culture is characterized by peace and love, its most powerful representative cannot change an unjust society.

Gerry's size represents his power, and this size is shown to contrast with the weighshack, and, therefore, with the society he is immersed in. The narrator describes Gerry as being "bigger than I remembered from the bar" (234). Gerry is "so big that he had to hunker one shoulder beneath the lintel and back his belly in, pushing the doorframe wider with his hands" (234). The narrator's description suggests not only that Gerry is big, but that his size is so extreme, it seems to defy reality and thus escapes the narrator's memory. He manages to fit through the door by some magical means, literally bending the doorframe and contorting himself to enter the weighshack. The weighshack, where Dot and the narrator are employed by a dishonest institution, represents the dominant culture around Dot and Gerry. Since

---

* Reproduced with permission of David Mongar.

it is seen as small in comparison to Gerry, the story suggests that, on some level, Gerry has greater power than that of society.

Through the description of the skill with which Gerry disarms Dot the passage emphasizes the depth of his power, which is almost magical. The narrator describes watching Gerry's hands: "His plump fingers looked so graceful and artistic against his smooth mass" (234). She refers to them as "agile," and says that they are used "prettily" (234). His littlest fingers curl, "like a woman's at tea" (234). All of these descriptions of Gerry's hands are unexpected; a man of such extreme size having such delicate hands suggests something strange, even magical. "Plump" fingers being "graceful" and "artistic" defy assumptions that large people tend to be clumsy and awkward. The descriptions of Gerry's hands as pretty and "like a woman's at tea" all allude to a tender, nurturing femininity, and contribute to the sense that Gerry has a magical power to be many things at once.

The way in which Gerry takes the knitting needles from Dot and his compliment of her work reveal that despite his power, Gerry has a peaceful, loving nature. The narrator describes Gerry's littlest fingers curling around Dot's knitting needles and "disarm[ing] his wife" by drawing the needles out of Dot's fists (234). There is a peace about this interaction that resonates with Gerry's peaceful struggle against violence. The narrator's description of Gerry as "disarming" Dot suggests that until Gerry arrives on the scene, the knitting needles are seen as weapons. The use of his "littlest fingers" implies that Gerry has no need to use force, that Dot's fists will offer him no resistance. Gerry says, "'S very, very nice," and scrutinizes the tiny stitches of the garment, which causes Dot to nod "solemnly" and drop her eyes to her lap. Gerry, in offering such a compliment of Dot's work, symbolically approves of her as a mother. Dot is clearly honoured by Gerry's loving acceptance, as she drops her eyes, showing her humility, both in regard to Gerry, and her duties as a mother.

The resolution of the conflict, in which Jason, the child of Dot and Gerry, is placed on the scale with monumental hope, but no effect, suggests that even a powerful minority that is peaceful and magical cannot bring about change in an unjust society. The story's depiction of Dot as a direct, resourceful, and abundant nurturer for her child, and Gerry as a magical, tender, and peaceful symbol of power elevates Jason to an extraordinary status. The union of these two beings creates such "a powerful distillation of Dot and Gerry" that the narrator states, "it seemed to me [Jason] might weigh as much as any load" (238). As Dot and the narrator prepare to place him on the scales, which represent the cultural balance within society, Jason, therefore, carries not only the hopes of his Native American people, but the hopes of all minorities that struggle for equality. That Gerry is a being of such magical power and that his struggle against the dominant culture is always non-threatening and peaceful, that the child is prepared for so dangerous a world by such a nurturing mother, and that he is conceived in impossible circumstances from a union of pure, tender love, however, is all without consequence. Gerry's arrest fractures the unity of their culture, and Jason is left to tip the scales by himself. He is described as being "dense with life" and he stares "calmly" into the rough sky ahead as he is placed on the scale. He bears the hope of many on his little shoulders, and yet is unable to effect change, unable to tip the scales. His failure to register clearly suggests the failure of everything he represents to change society.

In "Scales," the fate of Gerry, Dot, and their son seems to express pessimism about the ability of a minority, even one empowered by love and magic, to resist an unjust society. This essay has not considered the connections that might exist between Gerry's special powers and Native American myth. Such connections might suggest different conclusions about the permanence of Gerry's imprisonment and the story's theme.

Work Cited

Erdrich, Louise. "Scales." *Points of View: An Anthology of Short Stories.* Edited by James Moffett and Kenneth R. McElheny, rev. ed., Penguin, 1995, pp. 229–38.

\\ 7. A COMPARATIVE LITERARY ANALYSIS ESSAY*

Nguyen 1

Cheri Nguyen
Dr. Paul Headrick
English 2225
30 July 2007

Two Views of Sexual Desire: "The Cinnamon Peeler" and
"Violets for Your Furs"

Michael Ondaatje's "The Cinnamon Peeler" and George Elliot Clarke's "Violets for Your Furs" are challenging poems that deal with sexual love. Each poem uses rich figurative language to evoke a powerful sense of the force of sexual love. The attitudes they express, however, are quite different. "The Cinnamon Peeler" suggests that sexual love is positive, so much so that it is essential to who we are, whereas "Violets for Your Furs" implicitly argues that the power of sexual love is profoundly damaging.

The "cinnamon peeler" that the speaker imagines in Ondaatje's poem is a powerful symbol of sexual love. In the first stanza, the speaker wittily addresses his lover and says, "If I were a cinnamon peeler / I would ride your bed" (lines 1–2). The "ride" the speaker imagines, taking place as it does on the woman's bed, clearly is a sexual encounter. This first expression of what the speaker would do if he were a cinnamon peeler clearly establishes the power of his sexual desire and connects the desire to the spice. Being redolent of cinnamon is what would enable the speaker to fulfill his sexual desire. The speaker says that he must also "leave . . . yellow bark dust / on [her] pillow" (3–4). The yellow bark dust, which is cinnamon, is a symbol of their sexual love. The cinnamon left on the pillow is a sign of the persistent power of sexual love.

The speaker also imagines that the sexual connection with his lover is so powerful that it will establish her social identity. He says that she "will be known among strangers / as the cinnamon peeler's wife" (17–18). This line is repeated in the last stanza, emphasizing the idea that the speaker's sexual love is the making of his lover. He, the speaker imagines, would be defined by what he does, and what he does is established as sexual; she would be defined by her connection to his sexual identity—she would *be* the cinnamon peeler's wife.

George Elliot Clark's "Violets for Your Furs" also presents a picture of the power of sexual love, but that power is negative. In the first stanza, the speaker grieves for a departed lover. He still dreams of her (line 1) and he suffers "Cointreau's blues aftertaste of burnt orange / The torturous bitter flavour of the French in Africa" (3–4). Just as the power of sexual love is represented sensually in "The Cinnamon Peeler" by the bark powder, the persistence of the love between the speaker and his lover is represented in "Violets for Your Furs" sensually through the image of the aftertaste of cointreau, but that aftertaste evokes the "blues" and is "bitter." Most emphatically, the negative effects of the lover's departure are suggested by the comparison to the French in Africa. The image suggests that his lover's effect on him is, on a personal level, analogous to the effect of an exploitive colonial power on its colony, and the lover's departure has left him in the same damaged state, body and soul, as the departure of the colonizers leaves an exploited people.

Key words in "The Cinnamon Peeler" emphasize the powerful effects of sexual love. The speaker declares that his lover's "breasts and shoulders would reek" (5). The word "reek" clearly defines her as his lover; as he himself "reeks" of the scent of cinnamon, she would be unmistakably, physically his. The specific reference to his lover's breasts and shoulders conveys the impression of his having touched her intimately, and that having touched her he has made her be like him. With confidence, the speaker declares that not only would his lover reek of his smell, but she would reek so strongly that she "could never walk through the markets / without the profession of [his] fingers / floating over [her]" (6–8). Proudly, he claims that even "The blind" would recognize her regardless of whether she washed herself "under rain gutters, monsoon" (11). His statements show that his connection to her is powerful enough that anyone and everyone who passes would be able to identify her by her spicy scent. Not even monsoon, the natural forces of weather, could eliminate the strong odour, representing their sexual union, which has made her identifiably his.

Key words, repetition, and alliteration in "Violets for Your Furs" emphasize the negative effects of sexual love. In the second stanza, the speaker describes his lost love and the power she has had over him: "you were a living S, all Coltrane or Picasso swerves / Your hair stranded splendid on . . . your face / So sweet, I moaned black rum, black sax, black moon / The black trace of your eyelash like lightning" (9–12). The metaphor describes the lost love as a work of art, and not just the creation of any artist, for Coltrane and Picasso are each considered among the greatest in their respective fields. The description of her as a "living S" evokes an image of curves and suggests that his vision of her is governed by his feelings of sexual love. These images might seem positive, but the effect on the speaker is not so. The "ess" sounds in the words "stranded" and "splendid" and "face" connect to the description of the lover as an "S" and convey a sense of sexual obsession, an obsession that persists destructively after the lover has gone.

"The Cinnamon Peeler" suggests that sexual desire is itself desirable, that not to feel it is not to be fulfilled. In the fourth stanza, the speaker reminds his love how she was once "blind of smell" (30), to which she rhetorically asks, "what good is it / to be the lime burner's daughter / left with no trace / as if not spoken to in the act of love / as if wounded without the pleasure of a scar" (37–41). The woman laments for the women who have not been graced by the indelibility of sexual love. The lime burner's daughter, who has not been possessed in any way in the act of love-making, is without an identity. In the final stanza, the speaker addresses the woman who has become his wife, and says, "You touched / your belly to my hands / . . . and said / I am the cinnamon / peeler's wife. Smell me" (42–46). Here, the woman's statements make clear that she is proud to be the cinnamon peeler's wife. Her invitation to him suggests a sharing of power in their sexual union. He too should smell her.

The despairing tone of the speaker in "Violets for Your Furs" shifts in the final stanza, intensifying the impression the poem creates of sexual love as a damaging force. The speaker, still addressing his lover, says, "I can't sleep—haunted by sad sweetness" (17). The speaker is unable to sleep because he is caught between two senses: sadness and the "sweetness" of the memory of his lover. He recalls, "The hurtful perfume you bathed in by the yellow lamp . . . your rouged kiss branding my neck / The orange cry of my mouth kindling your blue night skin" (18–20). In each of these lines a word suggests pain or injury: "hurtful," "branding," "cry." The speaker then says, "The night blossoms ugly" (21). Clearly, he is so affected by his bitter, hopeless longing that his view of the world has been poisoned. He imagines the night-blooming flowers as "ugly." In several places in the poem the speaker refers to alcohol, and here, in the final stanza, he drinks "gilded damnation" (21). The speaker is conscious that he is damning himself, but can do nothing to stop himself; sexual love has damaged him so severely. The poem, thus, suggests that the effect of sexual love is physically and emotionally destructive. It can dominate one's life and destroy it.

The two poems do not simply tell different love stories; they present different pictures of sexual love, one insisting that failing to embrace it almost makes us less human, the other warning of its destructive power. It would be interesting to analyze the poems further, to consider their political contexts and the suggestions of the connections between sexual love and the politics of race.

Works Cited

Clarke, George Elliot. "Violets for Your Furs." 1994. *A New Anthology of Canadian Literature in English*, edited by Donna Bennett and Russell Brown, Oxford UP, 2002, pp. 1153–54.

Ondaatje, Michael. "The Cinnamon Peeler." 1982. *A New Anthology of Canadian Literature in English*, edited by Donna Bennett and Russell Brown, Oxford UP, 2002, pp. 892–84.

\\ 8. A LITERARY ANALYSIS RESEARCH ESSAY USING CRITICAL SOURCES

Sutherland 1

May Sutherland
Dr. Paul Headrick
ENGL 2237
February 17, 2004

Suspicious History: About the Ending of Graham Swift's *Waterland*

If there is one thing on which the text of *Waterland* insists, it is the messiness and uncertainty of history—not official History, in its textbook form, or even the unofficial history of tales and rumours, but the history that actually happens. Through most of the novel, the content and form of Tom Crick's narrative counteracts the tendency of history recorders to tidy things up, or, as Damon Marcel Decoste puts it, "to simplify, finalize, and even brutally exclude" (390). Historical narratives of all kinds are constructions, Crick tells us, and his own narrative foregrounds its constructedness, calling attention to the ways in which it fails legitimately to account for what really happened. In an important and ultimately undermining shift, however, the imagery of the novel's final chapter gives a tidy conclusion to an otherwise messy and inconclusive tale. History can indeed be contained and made sense of, the ending suggests, offering a form of satisfaction of which the Tom Crick of the rest of the novel would be suspicious.

Significantly, and somewhat paradoxically, Crick, the text's voice of moral and intellectual authority, does argue for a certain form of historical sense and tidiness in the workings of hubris. Hubris, Crick maintains, "provides that there can be no success with impunity, no great achievement without accompanying loss" (72). This belief in the existence of what might be called poetic justice suggests, on one level, that history is governed, and that it progresses toward particular ends, in accordance with laws—implicit in the term "impunity"—and plans. Recognizing the potential for this theory to be associated with "[s]ome supernatural power" (72), Crick naturalizes hubris by connecting it with water, "which, however much you coax it, this way and that, will return, at the slightest opportunity, to its former equilibrium" (72). Through this view of history as tending, like nature, to maintain a certain equilibrium, which acts against "unnatural" excesses (potent beer, incest), the fatalism and sense of order of the novel's ending might be viewed as consistent with what comes before.

Yet most of what comes before explicitly stresses the disorder and non-teleological character of history. Crick counters the notion that history progresses according to laws and plans with his wonderfully ironic remark about the French Revolution "simmering in Paris" (16) so that students would one day have a subject for their lessons. He invites his students (and readers) to forget "revolutions" and "grand metamorphoses of history" and to consider instead "the slow and arduous, the interminable and ambiguous process" that history really is (10). He instructs us not to "fall into the illusion that history is a well-disciplined and unflagging column marching unswervingly into the future" (135). For Crick, clearly, the ambiguous, never-ending unfolding of history—of life, of the real—resists the neat containment, in linear, conclusive narratives that chroniclers of revolutions and grand narratives, and, implicitly, of ordinary tales, would attempt to impose. Moreover, the unfolding of history corresponds, Crick suggests, to no particular design or end. It is undisciplined; it flags and swerves. There is, in effect, no predetermined meaning to events, no "future" toward which those events are destined.

The lack of discipline of history, of life, is emphasized not only in the content of *Waterland* but in its form as well. An appropriate reflection of the complexity and open-endedness of the reality it seeks to represent, Crick's narrative features temporal and situational juxtapositions, parenthetical explorations, and, as Robert K. Irish has pointed out, a general avoidance of closure (928). Through these formal features, Crick implicitly and metafictionally announces that his text cannot faithfully represent the history that is its subject. In order to illustrate the important implications of *Waterland*'s form, I will examine each feature in turn.

By juxtaposing different time frames and contexts, the text reinforces the idea that history is multidimensional, that it resists any notion of straightforward, authoritarian representation. Demonstrating the kinds of time shifts that characterize the entire novel, Crick says to his students, "Once, long ago, there was a future history teacher's wife who, though she said to the future history teacher they should never meet again, married him three years later" (122). And, in one of several juxtapositions of "ordinary" event and what Jean-François Lyotard calls "grand narrative" (xxiv), Crick explains that in "the late summer of 1940, while Hitler sets up shop in Paris and makes invasion plans," the young Tom Crick "rummages amongst the books his mother left behind her" (208). The first of these passages offers an arresting temporal jumble of "once," "long ago," "future," "history," "never," and "later," all within the narrative unit of a single sentence. The implication here is that each term is applicable, but each is relative: the "future" of one narrative moment is not that of another; the "never" attached to a particular event is not necessarily irrevocable. By forcing all of these temporal markers into the one sentence—just as several time frames coexist in the novel as a whole—Crick suggests that the selection of any particular temporal perspective in a narrative is arbitrary and will fail to exhaust the multitude of narrative possibilities. Likewise, a narrative that focuses on canonical History—the Nazi invasion of France, for instance—in favour of the multitude of other events occurring at the same time is no less an arbitrary and limiting construction than is the story of a young boy searching through his dead mother's belongings.

The novel further announces its own limitations with regard to the complexity of the real through recurring parenthetical asides. It is in the parentheses of the text that Crick ventures to tell the stories not told by his central narrative, to explain that which might conceivably have been left out: the fact that, when young Tom and Mary met, it was "sometimes merely to talk" (52); the notion that Crick's students have noticed "something just a bit edgy of late, something just a bit vulnerable about old Cricky" (138); the possibility that Ernest Atkinson's Home for war victims is a "gesture of revenge" (221). These "added" pieces of information seem initially to flesh out the narrative, to make it more complete, more accurate. But, paradoxically, the text's parenthetical explorations—the parentheses for which could often simply be left out of the sentence—function more importantly in the opposite way. Scattered throughout the narrative with a frequency that suggests the narrator is struggling to contain an uncontainable bulk of information, the novel's parenthetical asides serve as a further reminder that all cannot be accounted for.

More significant, perhaps, than Crick's penchant for the parenthetical is his avoidance, through ellipses and long dashes, of both syntactical and historical closure. Following Crick's account of Mary's attempted abortion, the young Tom—or perhaps the mature Tom—contemplates events in a series of unfinished thoughts of the sort that are found throughout the text: "Yes, I understand. Because if this baby had never . . . Then Dick would never . . . And Freddie . . . Because cause, effect . . . Because Mary said, I know what I'm going to . . . " (295). Although the reader is capable of filling in these elliptical blanks, their presence forestalls tidy conclusions by forcing a consideration of other possibilities. Similarly, the three semantic cousins, "because," "cause," and "effect," hovering on their own, call attention to themselves and to the very process of establishing causal relationships. Such a process is perhaps not as straightforward as we might think, Crick's unfinished explanations suggest. The effects we observe are not necessarily the result of the causes we surmise; nor, implicitly, are the phenomena that constitute those causes necessarily directed toward a particular end. Ultimately, the text suggests, the recorder of history is better off not attempting to provide tidy explanations at all.

It is the strength of this suggestion that makes the ending of *Waterland* inconsistent, even unsatisfying. For while the text has insisted, in a variety of ways, that history is undisciplined, non-teleological, and, above all, unrepresentable in any conclusive, authoritarian form, the novel's final chapter disregards these assertions. Even if we allow hubris a role in Dick's unfortunate end—the end of the Atkinsons—the scene at the dredger is far more orchestrated and conclusive than the rest of Crick's narrative would seem to allow. In considering the end of *Waterland*, I would disagree with Decoste's claim that the novel's conclusion, through Stan Booth's open-ended injunction, "undermines itself" (378), and argue instead that it is the rest of the novel that the conclusion subverts.

In the manner of a Hollywood adventure film, the scene at the dredger builds urgently but deliberately to a climax that is followed by a logical, closed resolution. The orchestrated urgency of the episode is conveyed by the felicitously assembled posse of men—Stan Booth, the USAAF aircraftmen, Tom and his father—rushing to save Dick, and by Henry Crick's desperate pleas: "Dick, it's all right! Dick. I'll be your father . . . " (356). Arguably, there is a certain amount of self-conscious irony in the text's treatment of the rescue mission and, in particular, of Nat and Joe, the eager aircraftmen. But this irony does not undermine the seriousness with which we are meant to read the chapter's progressively mounting tension.

When Tom calls, "Dick—don't do it!" (356), there is a powerful expectation, established by the audience of men, alongside whom the reader watches and waits, that, whether Dick jumps or not, there will be a dramatic climax, a show, of some kind.

And, indeed, Dick's plunge from the dredger and his ultimate disappearance are presented in theatrical and poetic terms:

> For a moment he perches, poises, teeters on the rail, the dull glow of the western sky behind him. And then he plunges. In a long, reaching powerful arc.. . . sufficiently reaching and powerful for us to observe his body, in its flight through the air, form a single, taut and seemingly limbless continuum . . . .
>
> And punctures the water, with scarcely a splash. And is gone. (357)

The imagery of this scene, which describes in striking alliteration the specific, athletic movements of Dick's body—the perching, the poising, the powerful plunge, the puncturing—and the romantic backdrop against which these movements are performed, suggests a deliberate act of choreography on the part of the narrator. The history represented by Crick's narrative corresponds, Crick suggests, teleologically, to a design, a purpose. The text implies here that the unfolding of its events has been as tidy and controlled as the "taut and seemingly limbless continuum" that Dick's body becomes. Moreover, that tidy unfolding of events has been directed toward an ending as inevitable as a diver's submersion, as totalizing as the water that closes over Dick with "scarcely a splash."

The sense of closure of *Waterland*'s ending comes not only from the dramatization of Dick's suicide but also from Crick's suggestion that the history that will succeed his narrative is fixed. Contradicting his earlier relativization of time and perspective, Crick declares that the information about his own and Mary's involvement in the murder of Freddie Parr is "a secret he and Mary will share for ever" (357). The implicit certainty of Crick's "for ever" contrasts sharply with his earlier observation that, although Mary once said she and Tom "should *never* meet again," she "married him three years later" (122; emphasis added). It would seem, in the former declaration, that Crick has abandoned his distrust of absolutes, and that he is asking his reader to accept with confidence the assurance that the incriminating details of Freddie's death will never be revealed. The two remarks can, of course, be seen to challenge and subvert each other; however, Crick's blunt "for ever," situated as it is in the novel's penultimate paragraph, holds greater sway. In light of this certainty, and in the wake of the dredger episode, the open-endedness of Stan Booth's appeal for an explanation is less powerful than Decoste suggests it is. Moreover, any challenge that Booth's "Someone best explain" (358) might have presented is subtly but thoroughly undermined by the novel's closing image.

By leaving the reader with the striking metonymic image of Dick's motorcycle, the text implies, contrary to its earlier declarations of inadequacy, that Crick's narrative is capable of representing, of standing in for, the history that actually happened. The metonymic connection between Dick and his motorbike is established early in the novel: whenever he has nothing else to do, "Dick works at his motor-bike. It could be said that Dick's love of machines, if love it is, springs from the fact that Dick himself is a sort of machine . . ." (38). Implicit here is a direct contiguity between Dick and the motorcycle. Through regularity of association, through Dick's "love," and even through ontological affinity, the motorcycle acquires the capacity to stand in for Dick. This metonymic relationship is called up to striking effect in the last sentence of the novel: "On the bank in the thickening dusk, in the will-o'-the-wisp dusk, abandoned but vigilant, a motor-cycle" (358). In terms of its implications, the content of this sentence is less significant than its figurative orientation. What the sentence suggests, as forcefully as the idea that it is Dick and all he represents standing vigilant on the bank, is that the relationship between Crick's now-complete narrative and the history with which it is metonymically connected is solid. The story is able to stand in for the history, the ending of *Waterland* finally claims.

If the question "Why?" implies, for Crick, "dissatisfaction, disquiet, a sense that all is not well" (106), then the ending of his narrative effectively stifles any "Whys" it might have left astir. It is an ending that disappoints through the very satisfaction it attempts to offer. Given that *Waterland* begins, appropriately, in the middle of one of Henry Crick's stories, a more suitable conclusion might have been the final line of Chapter 50: "Once upon a time—" (343).

Works Cited

Decoste, Damon Marcel. "Question and Apocalypse: The Endlessness of 'Historia' in Graham Swift's *Waterland.*" *Contemporary Literature*, vol. 43, no. 2, 2002, pp. 377–99.

Irish, Robert K. "'Let Me Tell You': About Desire and Narrativity in Graham Swift's *Waterland.*" *Modern Fiction Studies*, vol. 44, no. 4, 1998, pp. 917–34.

Lyotard, Jean-François. *The Postmodern Condition.* 1979. Translated by Geoff Bennington and Brian Massumi, Manchester UP, 1984.

Swift, Graham. *Waterland.* 1983. Vintage, 1998.

\\ 9. A LITERARY ANALYSIS RESEARCH ESSAY USING HISTORICAL SOURCES

Douglas McGeer
Dr. Paul Headrick
English 1128
November 24, 1997

Conformity and Evil in John Cheever's "The Five-Forty-Eight"

Among the issues raised in John Cheever's complicated and subtle story "The Five-Forty-Eight" is that of the relationship between conformity and morality. This is certainly not the story's only topic, but it is one that gains emphasis when the story is considered in its historical context—New York City of the early 1950s. Understood in this context, the story is not just a critique of its main character, Blake, but of the conformist society that he represents. An important theme of "The Five-Forty-Eight" is that a culture that mistakes superficial conformity for moral value is evil, in a way that is destructive for others and also self-destructive.

The United States in the early 1950s was marked by prosperity, but also by fear and conformity. The authors of *Modern Civilization* note that "The most obvious fact about the postwar United States was its prosperity" (Brinton, Christopher, and Wolff 822). The prosperity, however, did not mean that American life was without anxieties, for, as Morris Dickstein points out, "behind its material growth hover[ed] a quiet despair, whose symbols [were] the Bomb and the still-vivid death camps and a fear of Armageddon" (50). The fear of Armageddon was connected to the notorious "Red Scare" of the time, the fear that communists had infiltrated American life at all levels, including government. Dickstein describes how "the mania of national security . . . ruined the lives of some [and] touched many others with the cold hand of fear and conformity" (26–27). The novelist Norman Mailer, a leading intellectual in the United States of the fifties, wrote of the period that it produced "a slow death by conformity, with every creative and rebellious instinct stifled" (qtd. in Dickstein 53). To summarize the ethos of a complicated culture in a single paragraph is a perilous task; nevertheless, the agreement of these different commentators shows that the culture of America in the 1950s was prosperous, fearful, and conformist.

Blake represents his culture. He works near Madison Avenue, the heart of the business district in the city that is the heart of the American economy. He has enough authority to have a secretary and to have her fired by personnel merely on his say so (372). His place of work and the authority of his position establish his prosperity, one of the ways he parallels his culture. Blake obeys the "sumptuary laws" (373); that is, he dresses in a way that conforms to the pattern expected of him. The drink he orders is a Gibson. His choice of alcohol shows that his conformity extends even to small details, as a Gibson is a kind of martini, which "was the drink of the WASP upper class" (Passmore). Blake fears Miss Dent before he has any real reason to think she might be planning to do him harm. More subtly, but perhaps more importantly, the narrator suggests that Blake's conformity is a product of fear, noting that the "scrupulous lack of color in his clothing . . . seemed protective" (372). The story, then, suggests that Blake fears appearing to be different, fears the scrutiny such a distinction might invite. In his response to Miss Dent, and in his frightened conformity, Blake exemplifies his fearful culture. The narrator describes how, in his dispute with Watkins regarding Blake's son, "Mr. Watkins' long and dirty hair and his corduroy jacket reassured Blake that he had been in the right" (374). Blake, this observation makes clear, connects conformity with morality. He believes he has no need really to listen to Watkins or consider his position, because, having violated the conformist code of fashion of the business world to which Blake belongs, Watkins, Blake thinks, cannot possibly have right on his side. His harsh judgment of Watkins's nonconformity implies how much of a conformist Blake is, and, thus, how he represents his culture.

Blake's behaviour establishes him as immoral. He is, to put it mildly, cold to his wife and children and contemptuous of his neighbours. He sexually exploits women whom, the narrator says directly, he "picked for their lack of self esteem" (371). These behaviours are so widely considered worthy of condemnation that, in the absence of any contrary evidence, the story must be taken as critical of Blake as immoral.

Key imagery in the story suggests that the story sees Blake's immorality as evil. Blake is attracted to darkness in Miss Dent, and his entire world is dark. His sexual encounter with Miss Dent takes place in the dark, as it is only by the light from the slightly ajar bathroom door that he is able to read a note she has written (371). His clothing is dark (372). The light on the coach of the train he rides is "dim" (374), and the daylight through which it travels is "weak." Sunset provides a "dim firelight" before it is "put out" (376). The only interruptions in this unremitting darkness are provided by Miss Dent, who appears suddenly to Blake on two occasions. The first of these is on the street outside his office. Miss Dent appears behind Blake as he is looking in a shop window. Opposite them a building has been torn down, and the narrator notes that "daylight poured through the gap" (368). Her second sudden appearance is on the train, and it coincides with a "break in the clouds—a piece of yellow light" (374). Darkness is conventionally associated with evil, and light is conventionally associated with good, so Blake's emphatic connection to darkness, especially in contrast with Miss Dent, strongly suggests that he is evil.

The story's resolution suggests that the evil culture that Blake represents is not only damaging to others, but self-destructive as well. Blake brings cheer into his world through, as the narrator puts it, "calculated self deceptions" (379). The comment clearly implies that Blake *knows* something is wrong with him or his world, for he must, in a "calculated way," deceive himself in order for any happiness to come from it. He does not, however, try to end these deceptions and change. The culture, in other words, cannot claim ignorance; on some level it is aware of its deep problems, but it denies them. No one comes to Blake's aid as he rides the train, because he has alienated everyone who might otherwise notice something is wrong. His fear, his conformity, and his abuse of the power that comes with his prosperity have left him alone and vulnerable. At the station, no one arrives to pick up Blake, and no one offers assistance to him. By making Blake's helplessness a consequence of his alienating behaviour, the story suggests that the evil of the culture makes it vulnerable and self-destructive.

It is clear that the evil figure of Blake represents a fearful, conformist culture of which the story is harshly critical. This analysis has not considered what Miss Dent, a deceptively complex figure, might represent and what is meant by her apparent victory at the end of the story.

Works Cited

Brinton, Crane, John B. Christopher, and Robert Lee Wolff. *Modern Civilization: A History of the Last Five Centuries.* 2nd ed. Englewood Cliffs: Prentice-Hall, 1967. Print.

Cheever, John. "The Five-Forty-Eight." 1955. *Points of View: An Anthology of Short Stories.* Rev. ed. Ed. James Moffett and Kenneth R. McElheny. New York: Penguin, 1995. 368–82. Print.

Dickstein, Morris. *Gates of Eden: American Culture in the Sixties.* 1989 ed. New York: Penguin, 1979. Print.

Passmore, Nick. "In Praise of the Silver Bullet." *Forbes.com.* Forbes Magazine, 14 Mar. 2006. Web. 31 Oct. 1997.

"THE YELLOW WALLPAPER," BY CHARLOTTE PERKINS GILMAN (1860–1935)

It is very seldom that mere ordinary people like John and myself secure ancestral halls for the summer.

A colonial mansion, a hereditary estate, I would say a haunted house, and reach the height of romantic felicity—but that would be asking too much of fate!

Still I will proudly declare that there is something queer about it.

Else, why should it be let so cheaply? And why have stood so long untenanted?

John laughs at me, of course, but one expects that in marriage.

John is practical in the extreme. He has no patience with faith, an intense horror of superstition, and he scoffs openly at any talk of things not to be felt and seen and put down in figures.

John is a physician, and *perhaps*—(I would not say it to a living soul, of course, but this is dead paper and a great relief to my mind)—*perhaps* that is one reason I do not get well faster.

You see he does not believe I am sick!

And what can one do?

If a physician of high standing, and one's own husband, assures friends and relatives that there is really nothing the matter with one but temporary nervous depression—a slight hysterical tendency—what is one to do?

My brother is also a physician, and also of high standing, and he says the same thing.

So I take phosphates or phosphites—whichever it is, and tonics, and journeys, and air, and exercise, and am absolutely forbidden to "work" until I am well again. Personally, I disagree with their ideas.

Personally, I believe that congenial work, with excitement and change, would do me good.

But what is one to do?

I did write for a while in spite of them; but it does exhaust me a good deal—having to be so sly about it, or else meet with heavy opposition.

I sometimes fancy that in my condition if I had less opposition and more society and stimulus—but John says the very worst thing I can do is to think about my condition, and I confess it always makes me feel bad.

So I will let it alone and talk about the house.

The most beautiful place! It is quite alone standing well back from the road, quite three miles from the village. It makes me think of English places that you read about, for there are hedges and walls and gates that lock, and lots of separate little houses for the gardeners and people.

There is a *delicious* garden! I never saw such a garden—large and shady, full of box-bordered paths, and lined with long grape-covered arbors with seats under them.

There were greenhouses, too, but they are all broken now.

There was some legal trouble, I believe, something about the heirs and coheirs; anyhow, the place has been empty for years.

That spoils my ghostliness, I am afraid, but I don't care—there is something strange about the house—I can feel it.

I even said so to John one moonlight evening but he said what I felt was a *draught,* and shut the window.

I get unreasonably angry with John sometimes. I'm sure I never used to be so sensitive. I think it is due to this nervous condition.

But John says if I feel so, I shall neglect proper self-control; so I take pains to control myself—before him, at least, and that makes me very tired.

I don't like our room a bit. I wanted one downstairs that opened on the piazza and had roses all over the window, and such pretty old-fashioned chintz hangings! but John would not hear of it.

He said there was only one window and not room for two beds, and no near room for him if he took another.

He is very careful and loving, and hardly lets me stir without special direction.

I have a schedule prescription for each hour in the day; he takes all care from me, and so I feel basely ungrateful not to value it more.

He said we came here solely on my account, that I was to have perfect rest and all the air I could get. "Your exercise depends on your strength, my dear," said he, "and your food somewhat on your appetite; but air you can absorb all the time." So we took the nursery at the top of the house.

It is a big, airy room, the whole floor nearly, with windows that look all ways, and air and sunshine galore. It was nursery first and then playroom and gymnasium, I should judge; for the windows are barred for little children, and there are rings and things in the walls.

The paint and paper look as if a boys' school had used it. It is stripped off—the paper in great patches all around the head of my bed, about as far as I can reach, and in a great place on the other side of the room low down. I never saw a worse paper in my life.

One of those sprawling flamboyant patterns committing every artistic sin.

It is dull enough to confuse the eye in following, pronounced enough to constantly irritate and provoke study, and when you follow the lame uncertain curves for a little distance they suddenly commit suicide—plunge off at outrageous angles, destroy themselves in unheard of contradictions.

The color is repellent, almost revolting; a smouldering unclean yellow, strangely faded by the slow-turning sunlight.

It is a dull yet lurid orange in some places, a sickly sulphur tint in others.

No wonder the children hated it! I should hate it myself if I had to live in this room long.

There comes John, and I must put this away,—he hates to have me write a word.

We have been here two weeks, and I haven't felt like writing before, since that first day.

I am sitting by the window now, up in this atrocious nursery, and there is nothing to hinder my writing as much as I please, save lack of strength.

John is away all day, and even some nights when his cases are serious.

I am glad my case is not serious!

But these nervous troubles are dreadfully depressing.

John does not know how much I really suffer. He knows there is no *reason* to suffer, and that satisfies him.

Of course it is only nervousness. It does weigh on me so not to do my duty in any way!

I meant to be such a help to John, such a real rest and comfort, and here I am a comparative burden already!

Nobody would believe what an effort it is to do what little I am able,—to dress and entertain, and order things.

It is fortunate Mary is so good with the baby. Such a dear baby!

And yet I *cannot* be with him, it makes me so nervous.

I suppose John never was nervous in his life. He laughs at me so about this wall-paper!

At first he meant to repaper the room, but afterwards he said that I was letting it get the better of me, and that nothing was worse for a nervous patient than to give way to such fancies.

He said that after the wall-paper was changed it would be the heavy bedstead, and then the barred windows, and then that gate at the head of the stairs, and so on.

"You know the place is doing you good," he said, "and really, dear, I don't care to renovate the house just for a three months' rental."

"Then do let us go downstairs," I said, "there are such pretty rooms there."

Then he took me in his arms and called me a blessed little goose, and said he would go down cellar, if I wished, and have it whitewashed into the bargain.

But he is right enough about the beds and windows and things.

It is an airy and comfortable room as any one need wish, and, of course, I would not be so silly as to make him uncomfortable just for a whim.

I'm really getting quite fond of the big room, all but that horrid paper.

Out of one window I can see the garden, those mysterious deep-shaded arbors, the riotous old-fashioned flowers, and bushes and gnarly trees.

Out of another I get a lovely view of the bay and a little private wharf belonging to the estate. There is a beautiful shaded lane that runs down there from the house. I always fancy I see people walking in these numerous paths and arbors, but John has cautioned me not to give way to fancy in the least. He says that with my imaginative power and habit of story-making, a nervous weakness like mine is sure to lead to all manner of excited fancies, and that I ought to use my will and good sense to check the tendency. So I try.

I think sometimes that if I were only well enough to write a little it would relieve the press of ideas and rest me.

But I find I get pretty tired when I try.

It is so discouraging not to have any advice and companionship about my work. When I get really well, John says we will ask Cousin Henry and Julia down for a long visit; but he says he would as soon put fireworks in my pillow-case as to let me have those stimulating people about now.

I wish I could get well faster.

But I must not think about that. This paper looks to me as if it *knew* what a vicious influence it had!

There is a recurrent spot where the pattern lolls like a broken neck and two bulbous eyes stare at you upside down.

I get positively angry with the impertinence of it and the everlastingness. Up and down and sideways they crawl, and those absurd, unblinking eyes are everywhere. There is one place where two breadths didn't match, and the eyes go all up and down the line, one a little higher than the other.

I never saw so much expression in an inanimate thing before, and we all know how much expression they have! I used to lie awake as a child and get more entertainment and terror out of blank walls and plain furniture than most children could find in a toy-store.

I remember what a kindly wink the knobs of our big, old bureau used to have, and there was one chair that always seemed like a strong friend.

I used to feel that if any of the other things looked too fierce I could always hop into that chair and be safe.

The furniture in this room is no worse than inharmonious, however, for we had to bring it all from downstairs. I suppose when this was used as a playroom they had to take the nursery things out, and no wonder! I never saw such ravages as the children have made here.

The wall-paper, as I said before, is torn off in spots, and it sticketh closer than a brother—they must have had perseverance as well as hatred.

Then the floor is scratched and gouged and splintered, the plaster itself is dug out here and there, and this great heavy bed which is all we found in the room, looks as if it had been through the wars.

But I don't mind it a bit—only the paper.

There comes John's sister. Such a dear girl as she is, and so careful of me! I must not let her find me writing.

She is a perfect and enthusiastic housekeeper, and hopes for no better profession. I verily believe she thinks it is the writing which made me sick!

But I can write when she is out, and see her a long way off from these windows.

There is one that commands the road, a lovely shaded winding road, and one that just looks off over the country. A lovely country, too, full of great elms and velvet meadows.

This wall-paper has a kind of sub-pattern in a different shade, a particularly irritating one, for you can only see it in certain lights, and not clearly then.

But in the places where it isn't faded and where the sun is just so—I can see a strange, provoking, formless sort of figure, that seems to skulk about behind that silly and conspicuous front design.

There's sister on the stairs!

Well, the Fourth of July is over! The people are all gone and I am tired out. John thought it might do me good to see a little company, so we just had mother and Nellie and the children down for a week.

Of course I didn't do a thing. Jennie sees to everything now.

But it tired me all the same.

John says if I don't pick up faster he shall send me to Weir Mitchell in the fall.

But I don't want to go there at all. I had a friend who was in his hands once, and she says he is just like John and my brother, only more so!

Besides, it is such an undertaking to go so far.

I don't feel as if it was worth while to turn my hand over for anything, and I'm getting dreadfully fretful and querulous.

I cry at nothing, and cry most of the time.

Of course I don't when John is here, or anybody else, but when I am alone.

And I am alone a good deal just now. John is kept in town very often by serious cases, and Jennie is good and lets me alone when I want her to.

So I walk a little in the garden or down that lovely lane, sit on the porch under the roses, and lie down up here a good deal.

I'm getting really fond of the room in spite of the wall-paper. Perhaps *because* of the wall-paper.

It dwells in my mind so!

I lie here on this great immovable bed—it is nailed down, I believe—and follow that pattern about by the hour. It is as good as gymnastics, I assure you. I start, we'll say, at the bottom, down in the corner over there where it has not been touched, and I determine for the thousandth time that I *will* follow that pointless pattern to some sort of a conclusion.

I know a little of the principle of design, and I know this thing was not arranged on any laws of radiation, or alternation, or repetition, or symmetry, or anything else that I ever heard of.

It is repeated, of course, by the breadths, but not otherwise.

Looked at in one way each breadth stands alone, the bloated curves and flourishes—a kind of "debased Romanesque" with *delirium tremens*—go waddling up and down in isolated columns of fatuity.

But, on the other hand, they connect diagonally, and the sprawling outlines run off in great slanting waves of optic horror, like a lot of wallowing seaweeds in full chase.

The whole thing goes horizontally, too, at least it seems so, and I exhaust myself in trying to distinguish the order of its going in that direction.

They have used a horizontal breadth for a frieze, and that adds wonderfully to the confusion.

There is one end of the room where it is almost intact, and there, when the cross-lights fade and the low sun shines directly upon it, I can almost fancy radiation after all,—the interminable grotesques seem to form around a common centre and rush off in headlong plunges of equal distraction.

It makes me tired to follow it. I will take a nap I guess.

I don't know why I should write this.

I don't want to.

I don't feel able. And I know John would think it absurd. But I must say what I feel and think in some way—it is such a relief!

But the effort is getting to be greater than the relief.

Half the time now I am awfully lazy, and lie down ever so much.

John says I mustn't lose my strength, and has me take cod liver oil and lots of tonics and things, to say nothing of ale and wine and rare meat.

Dear John! He loves me very dearly, and hates to have me sick. I tried to have a real earnest reasonable talk with him the other day, and tell him how I wish he would let me go and make a visit to Cousin Henry and Julia.

But he said I wasn't able to go, nor able to stand it after I got there; and I did not make out a very good case for myself, for I was crying before I had finished.

It is getting to be a great effort for me to think straight. Just this nervous weakness I suppose.

And dear John gathered me up in his arms, and just carried me upstairs and laid me on the bed, and sat by me and read to me till it tired my head.

He said I was his darling and his comfort and all he had, and that I must take care of myself for his sake, and keep well.

He says no one but myself can help me out of it, that I must use my will and self-control and not let any silly fancies run away with me.

There's one comfort, the baby is well and happy, and does not have to occupy this nursery with the horrid wall-paper.

If we had not used it, that blessed child would have! What a fortunate escape! Why, I wouldn't have a child of mine, an impressionable little thing, live in such a room for worlds.

I never thought of it before, but it is lucky that John kept me here after all, I can stand it so much easier than a baby, you see.

Of course I never mention it to them any more—I am too wise,—but I keep watch of it all the same.

There are things in that paper that nobody knows but me, or ever will.

Behind that outside pattern the dim shapes get clearer every day.

It is always the same shape, only very numerous.

And it is like a woman stooping down and creeping about behind that pattern. I don't like it a bit. I wonder—I begin to think—I wish John would take me away from here!

It is so hard to talk with John about my case, because he is so wise, and because he loves me so.

But I tried it last night.

It was moonlight. The moon shines in all around just as the sun does.

I hate to see it sometimes, it creeps so slowly, and always comes in by one window or another.

John was asleep and I hated to waken him, so I kept still and watched the moonlight on that undulating wall-paper till I felt creepy.

The faint figure behind seemed to shake the pattern, just as if she wanted to get out.

I got up softly and went to feel and see if the paper *did* move, and when I came back John was awake.

"What is it, little girl?" he said. "Don't go walking about like that—you'll get cold."

I thought it was a good time to talk, so I told him that I really was not gaining here, and that I wished he would take me away.

"Why darling!" said he, "our lease will be up in three weeks, and I can't see how to leave before.

"The repairs are not done at home, and I cannot possibly leave town just now. Of course if you were in any danger, I could and would, but you really are better, dear, whether you can see it or not. I am a doctor, dear, and I know. You are gaining flesh and color, your appetite is better, I feel really much easier about you."

"I don't weigh a bit more," said I, "nor as much; and my appetite may be better in the evening when you are here, but it is worse in the morning when you are away!"

"Bless her little heart!" said he with a big hug, "she shall be as sick as she pleases! But now let's improve the shining hours by going to sleep, and talk about it in the morning!"

"And you won't go away?" I asked gloomily.

"Why, how can I, dear? It is only three weeks more and then we will take a nice little trip of a few days while Jennie is getting the house ready. Really dear you are better!"

"Better in body perhaps—" I began, and stopped short, for he sat up straight and looked at me with such a stern, reproachful look that I could not say another word.

"My darling," said he, "I beg of you, for my sake and for our child's sake, as well as for your own, that you will never for one instant let that idea enter your mind! There is nothing so dangerous, so fascinating, to a temperament like yours. It is a false and foolish fancy. Can you not trust me as a physician when I tell you so?"

So of course I said no more on that score, and we went to sleep before long. He thought I was asleep first, but I wasn't, and lay there for hours trying to decide whether that front pattern and the back pattern really did move together or separately.

On a pattern like this, by daylight, there is a lack of sequence, a defiance of law, that is a constant irritant to a normal mind.

The color is hideous enough, and unreliable enough, and infuriating enough, but the pattern is torturing.

You think you have mastered it, but just as you get well underway in following, it turns a back somersault and there you are. It slaps you in the face, knocks you down, and tramples upon you. It is like a bad dream.

The outside pattern is a florid arabesque, reminding one of a fungus. If you can imagine a toadstool in joints, an interminable string of toadstools, budding and sprouting in endless convolutions—why, that is something like it.

That is, sometimes!

There is one marked peculiarity about this paper, a thing nobody seems to notice but myself, and that is that it changes as the light changes.

When the sun shoots in through the east window—I always watch for that first long, straight ray—it changes so quickly that I never can quite believe it.

That is why I watch it always.

By moonlight—the moon shines in all night when there is a moon—I wouldn't know it was the same paper.

At night in any kind of light, in twilight, candlelight, lamplight, and worst of all by moonlight, it becomes bars! The outside pattern I mean, and the woman behind it is as plain as can be.

I didn't realize for a long time what the thing was that showed behind, that dim sub-pattern, but now I am quite sure it is a woman.

By daylight she is subdued, quiet. I fancy it is the pattern that keeps her so still. It is so puzzling. It keeps me quiet by the hour.

I lie down ever so much now. John says it is good for me, and to sleep all I can.

Indeed he started the habit by making me lie down for an hour after each meal.

It is a very bad habit I am convinced, for you see I don't sleep.

And that cultivates deceit, for I don't tell them I'm awake—O no!

The fact is I am getting a little afraid of John.

He seems very queer sometimes, and even Jennie has an inexplicable look.

It strikes me occasionally, just as a scientific hypothesis,—that perhaps it is the paper!

I have watched John when he did not know I was looking, and come into the room suddenly on the most innocent excuses, and I've caught him several times *looking at the paper*! And Jennie too. I caught Jennie with her hand on it once.

She didn't know I was in the room, and when I asked her in a quiet, a very quiet voice, with the most restrained manner possible, what she was doing with the paper— she turned around as if she had been caught stealing, and looked quite angry—asked me why I should frighten her so!

Then she said that the paper stained everything it touched, that she had found yellow smooches on all my clothes and John's, and she wished we would be more careful!

Did not that sound innocent? But I know she was studying that pattern, and I am determined that nobody shall find it out but myself!

Life is very much more exciting now than it used to be. You see I have something more to expect, to look forward to, to watch. I really do eat better, and am more quiet than I was.

John is so pleased to see me improve! He laughed a little the other day, and said I seemed to be flourishing in spite of my wall-paper.

I turned it off with a laugh. I had no intention of telling him it was *because* of the wall-paper—he would make fun of me. He might even want to take me away.

I don't want to leave now until I have found it out. There is a week more, and I think that will be enough.

I'm feeling ever so much better! I don't sleep much at night, for it is so interesting to watch developments; but I sleep a good deal in the daytime.

In the daytime it is tiresome and perplexing.

There are always new shoots on the fungus, and new shades of yellow all over it. I cannot keep count of them, though I have tried conscientiously.

It is the strangest yellow, that wall-paper! It makes me think of all the yellow things I ever saw—not beautiful ones like buttercups, but old foul, bad yellow things.

But there is something else about that paper—the smell! I noticed it the moment we came into the room, but with so much air and sun it was not bad. Now we have had a week of fog and rain, and whether the windows are open or not, the smell is here.

It creeps all over the house.

I find it hovering in the dining-room, skulking in the parlor, hiding in the hall, lying in wait for me on the stairs.

It gets into my hair.

Even when I go to ride, if I turn my head suddenly and surprise it—there is that smell!

Such a peculiar odor, too! I have spent hours in trying to analyze it, to find what it smelled like.

It is not bad—at first, and very gentle, but quite the subtlest, most enduring odor I ever met.

In this damp weather it is awful, I wake up in the night and find it hanging over me.

It used to disturb me at first. I thought seriously of burning the house—to reach the smell.

But now I am used to it. The only thing I can think of that it is like is the *color* of the paper! A yellow smell.

There is a very funny mark on this wall, low down, near the mopboard. A streak that runs round the room. It goes behind every piece of furniture, except the bed, a long, straight, even *smooch,* as if it had been rubbed over and over.

I wonder how it was done and who did it, and what they did it for. Round and round and round—round and round and round—it makes me dizzy!

I really have discovered something at last.

Through watching so much at night, when it changes so, I have finally found out.

The front pattern *does* move—and no wonder! The woman behind shakes it!

Sometimes I think there are a great many women behind, and sometimes only one, and she crawls around fast, and her crawling shakes it all over.

Then in the very bright spots she keeps still, and in the very shady spots she just takes hold of the bars and shakes them hard.

And she is all the time trying to climb through. But nobody could climb through that pattern—it strangles so; I think that is why it has so many heads.

They get through, and then the pattern strangles them off and turns them upside down, and makes their eyes white!

If those heads were covered or taken off it would not be half so bad.

I think that woman gets out in the daytime!

And I'll tell you why—privately—I've seen her!

I can see her out of every one of my windows!

It is the same woman, I know, for she is always creeping, and most women do not creep by daylight.

I see her on that long road under the trees, creeping along, and when a carriage comes she hides under the blackberry vines.

I don't blame her a bit. It must be very humiliating to be caught creeping by daylight!

I always lock the door when I creep by daylight. I can't do it at night, for I know John would suspect something at once.

And John is so queer now, that I don't want to irritate him. I wish he would take another room! Besides, I don't want anybody to get that woman out at night but myself.

I often wonder if I could see her out of all the windows at once.

But, turn as fast as I can, I can only see out of one at one time.

And though I always see her, she *may* be able to creep faster than I can turn!

I have watched her sometimes away off in the open country, creeping as fast as a cloud shadow in a high wind.

If only that top pattern could be gotten off from the under one! I mean to try it, little by little.

I have found out another funny thing, but I shan't tell it this time! It does not do to trust people too much.

There are only two more days to get this paper off, and I believe John is beginning to notice. I don't like the look in his eyes.

And I heard him ask Jennie a lot of professional questions about me. She had a very good report to give.

She said I slept a good deal in the daytime.

John knows I don't sleep very well at night, for all I'm so quiet!

He asked me all sorts of questions, too, and pretended to be very loving and kind.

As if I couldn't see through him!

Still, I don't wonder he acts so, sleeping under this paper for three months.

It only interests me, but I feel sure John and Jennie are secretly affected by it.

Hurrah! This is the last day, but it is enough. John to stay in town over night, and won't be out until this evening.

Jennie wanted to sleep with me—the sly thing! but I told her I should undoubtedly rest better for a night all alone.

That was clever, for really I wasn't alone a bit! As soon as it was moonlight and that poor thing began to crawl and shake the pattern, I got up and ran to help her.

I pulled and she shook, I shook and she pulled, and before morning we had peeled off yards of that paper.

A strip about as high as my head and half around the room.

And then when the sun came and that awful pattern began to laugh at me, I declared I would finish it to-day!

We go away to-morrow, and they are moving all my furniture down again to leave things as they were before.

Jennie looked at the wall in amazement, but I told her merrily that I did it out of pure spite at the vicious thing.

She laughed and said she wouldn't mind doing it herself, but I must not get tired.

How she betrayed herself that time!

But I am here, and no person touches this paper but me—not *alive*!

She tried to get me out of the room—it was too patent! But I said it was so quiet and empty and clean now that I believed I would lie down again and sleep all I could; and not to wake me even for dinner—I would call when I woke.

So now she is gone, and the servants are gone, and the things are gone, and there is nothing left but that great bedstead nailed down, with the canvas mattress we found on it.

We shall sleep downstairs to-night, and take the boat home to-morrow.

I quite enjoy the room, now it is bare again.

How those children did tear about here!

This bedstead is fairly gnawed!

But I must get to work.

I have locked the door and thrown the key down into the front path.

I don't want to go out, and I don't want to have anybody come in, till John comes.

I want to astonish him.

I've got a rope up here that even Jennie did not find. If that woman does get out, and tries to get away, I can tie her!

But I forgot I could not reach far without anything to stand on!

This bed will *not* move!

I tried to lift and push it until I was lame, and then I got so angry I bit off a little piece at one corner—but it hurt my teeth.

Then I peeled off all the paper I could reach standing on the floor. It sticks horribly and the pattern just enjoys it! All those strangled heads and bulbous eyes and waddling fungus growths just shriek with derision!

I am getting angry enough to do something desperate. To jump out of the window would be admirable exercise, but the bars are too strong even to try.

Besides I wouldn't do it. Of course not. I know well enough that a step like that is improper and might be misconstrued.

I don't like to *look* out of the windows even—there are so many of those creeping women, and they creep so fast.

I wonder if they all come out of that wall-paper as I did?

But I am securely fastened now by my well-hidden rope—you don't get *me* out in the road there!

I suppose I shall have to get back behind the pattern when it comes night, and that is hard!

It is so pleasant to be out in this great room and creep around as I please!

I don't want to go outside. I won't, even if Jennie asks me to.

For outside you have to creep on the ground, and everything is green instead of yellow.

But here I can creep smoothly on the floor, and my shoulder just fits in that long smooch around the wall, so I cannot lose my way.

Why there's John at the door!

It is no use, young man, you can't open it!

How he does call and pound!

Now he's crying for an axe.

It would be a shame to break down that beautiful door!

"John dear!" said I in the gentlest voice, "the key is down by the front steps, under a plantain leaf!"

That silenced him for a few moments.

Then he said—very quietly indeed, "Open the door, my darling!"

"I can't," said I. "The key is down by the front door under a plantain leaf!"

And then I said it again, several times, very gently and slowly, and said it so often that he had to go and see, and he got it of course, and came in. He stopped short by the door.

"What is the matter?" he cried. "For God's sake, what are you doing!"

I kept on creeping just the same, but I looked at him over my shoulder.

"I've got out at last," said I, "in spite of you and Jane. And I've pulled off most of the paper, so you can't put me back!"

Now why should that man have fainted? But he did, and right across my path by the wall, so that I had to creep over him every time!

EXERCISE 1.1 A

1. No. The sentence identifies the author's response to the poem, which is not of interest to an audience that is concerned with the poem's meaning.

2. No. The sentence evaluates the poem. The audience that is concerned with the poem's meaning, not with an evaluation of it.

3. No. The sentence summarizes part of the poem, and the audience has already understood the poem on this level. The sentence could be of interest, however, if it is not obvious that the speaker is doing what is described or if the sentence is presenting evidence that will then be analyzed.

4. No. The biographical detail is not related to the meaning of the poem.

5. Yes. The connection the poem makes between enlightenment and dispensing with worldly desire is not stated directly.

EXERCISE 2.1 A

1. Not analytical. The observation that the narrator is isolated summarizes obvious features of her situation.

2. Analytical. The claim points to something that is not stated directly in the story but rather is suggested indirectly.

3. Not analytical. The statement summarizes part of the story's plot.

4. Analytical. What the sister-in-law represents is not stated directly.

5. Analytical. The connection between the descriptions of the wallpaper and the narrator's inner life is not stated directly.

EXERCISE 2.2 A

1. Appropriate. The sentence presents evidence in the form of a properly integrated quotation.

2. Inappropriate. The sentence begins with analysis that should be included in a sentence following the evidence.

3. Inappropriate. The sentence ends with analysis, which should be included in a separate sentence following the evidence.

\\ EXERCISE 2.3 A

(Note that the underlined passages pertain to Exercise 2.5 A, question 3, below.)

CLAIM:

The narrator's reaction to the room in which she is staying suggests that she has been affected by her husband's attitude toward her, but she resists that attitude.

EVIDENCE:

She guesses at the history of the room: "It was nursery first and then playroom and gymnasium, I should judge; for the windows are barred for little children, and there are rings and things in the walls" (131). [1] She also notes that the wallpaper has been stripped from portions of the walls, that the floor has been "scratched and gouged and splintered" (134) and that the bed, it seems, has been nailed down (134). [2]

ANALYSIS:

These descriptions suggest a high degree of security [1] and also desperation in the room's former occupants. [2] The impression is more consistent with an asylum of some sort rather than a nursery. [1,2] *The narrator's sense that the room was used for children,* therefore, shows that she has been affected by her husband's attitude, and expects that the place she will be assigned is that of a child. [1,2]

EVIDENCE:

At the same time, however, she says, "I don't like our room a bit" (131). [3]

ANALYSIS:

Her resistance to the room shows that she resists her husband's effort to reduce her to a child. [3]

1. The claim, evidence, and analysis sections of the paragraph are identified above.

2. The numbers in square brackets in the evidence section follow each piece of evidence.

3. The numbers in square brackets in the analysis section refer to the evidence being analyzed in the previous phrase or sentence.

4. Yes

5. Affected, attitude, resists

6. The phrases that refer directly to the evidence are in italics in the analysis section.

7. Structure 2

\\ EXERCISE 2.4 A

There are many ways in which the analysis in question 1 and the claim in question 2 could be worded. Here are examples for each:

1. The narrator's attribution of specific feelings to the curves in the pattern of the wallpaper itself suggests that her mental state is at least unusual. People, obviously, do not ordinarily think of inanimate things such as wallpaper as having feelings, and the narrator seems to be describing the wallpaper in literal, not figurative terms. The feelings themselves seem to be a projection of her own "lame uncertain" state, which is indeed ominously fragile, as her description goes on to suggest that she may be contemplating suicide. The description of the colour of the paper, and the narrator's response to it hint at her sense of the evil that threatens her. The yellow paper is "smouldering," a word that is often used to describe anger that is ready to burst out, or any hot thing that is at a point that is potentially explosive. The "sickly sulphur" tint in the paper evokes hell, as the smell of sulphur is typically associated with Satan, an embodiment of evil. The description implies that the narrator is endangered by an evil that threatens to erupt and damage her.

2. Two important instances of personification suggest that the speaker feels that desire and lack of desire are forces that are separate from her, with desire being hostile, and lack of desire being good.

\\ EXERCISE 2.5 A

1. None. Quotations must be integrated into larger sentences.

2. Present tense

3. The phrases are underlined in the paragraph in the answer to Exercise 2.3 A.

4. The first sentence that presents evidence

5. A colon

\\ EXERCISE 3.1 A

1. No (c)

2. No (a)

3. No (a)

4. No (a)

5. No (b)

6. Yes

7. Yes

8. No (c)

9. No (a)

10. Yes

\\ EXERCISE 4.1 A

1. Yes. The claims are not logically connected and do not need to be in any specific sequence.

2. No. Changing the order of the claims disrupts the logical sequence.

3. Imagination, irrepressible, stifle, destructive

4. Imagination, stifle, irrepressibility, destructive

5. People, resist, dangerous, tendency, separate, nature

\\ EXERCISE 4.2 A

1. **Opening:** One of the topics of Alex B. Rankin's novel *Brilliantine* is love.

   Evidence Preview: Several key images in the novel...

   Link between the Evidence and the Thesis: ... are important to one of its main themes.

   Thesis: This main theme is that the idea of true love is a destructive illusion.

2. Love

3. Love

\\ EXERCISE 4.3 A

1. **Review:** It is clear, then, that the characters believe that they feel love. It is also evident that in the world of the novel, their love is considered "true."

   Preview: It is now necessary to show that this love is actually revealed to be an illusion, not to contrast it with feelings that are more genuine, but to show that the novel suggests that true love is always illusory.

2. Love, true, illusion

\\ EXERCISE 4.4 A

1. **The Summary:** True love is never really true, *Brilliantine* asks us to believe. The novel suggests that if we think this illusion is real, our lives will suffer for it.

   The New Possibility: Perhaps by questioning love the novel questions all of our most important values and asks whether our unthinking acceptance of them is dangerous.

   The Acknowledgment of Limitation: Much more than the novel's imagery could be analyzed to investigate this idea, as well as other topics this essay has not considered, such as the novel's attitude to the tension between the individual and the community.

2. True, love, illusion

\\ EXERCISE 4.5 A

Note that each title gives the title of the work being analyzed, the author of that work, and an abstract topic.

1. Love in Alex B. Rankin's *Brilliantine*

2. The Illusion of Love: An Analysis of Alex B. Rankin's *Brilliantine*

3. The Destructive Illusion: An Analysis of Love in Alex B. Rankin's *Brilliantine*

\\ EXERCISE 5.1 A

1. Minority, culture, peace, love, powerful, representative, change, unjust, society

2. Power, society

3. Power

4. The passage being analyzed

5. The passage being analyzed

\\ EXERCISE 5.2 A

1. **Opening:** Alex B. Rankin's novel *Brilliantine* and Davinder Lee's novel *Of Arrangements* are both about the destructive effects of the illusion of love.

   Key Difference or Similarity: While the two novels may seem to be dramatizing similar notions about the damage we do by holding to an illusion of love's reality, considering the texts together reveals a subtle but important contrast in what they imply about the significance of the unreality of love.

Evidence Preview: Through its depiction of those characters who seek an alternative to love,

Link between the Evidence and the Thesis: The link is made in the phrasing of the previous clause, beginning with the word "through," and in the parallel phrase later in the sentence: "also through the depictions of the characters who reject love."

Thesis: *Brilliantine* suggests that we can find ways other than through love to bring meaning into our lives and our cultures, ways that are more honest and fulfilling, while *Of Arrangements*, also through the depictions of the characters who reject love, makes the bleak argument that any attempt to centre our selves or our cultures leads us to accept destructive illusions that undermine our lives.

2. Destructive, illusion, love

3. Destructive, illusion, love

\\ EXERCISE 5.3 A

1. The critics make a general statement that establishes the background of a more specific argument. In this case, the more specific argument extends the logic of the critics' positions.

2. The introduction argues with the statement by the critic. The critic's statement is used to show that the essay's position is new.

3. The critic makes a general statement that is applied to the specific argument to strengthen its credibility and show that the specific argument is developing the critic's idea further.

\\ EXERCISE 5.4 A

1. The historical sources establish the ethos of a specific culture, that of the United States in the 1950s.

2. The historical source establishes the significance of a small detail in the text that might otherwise be overlooked.

GLOSSARY OF LITERARY TERMS

The following is a very brief glossary of terms that are useful to understand when writing literary analysis essays. There are many good literary glossaries and dictionaries available that include more terms and more extensive definitions. You are likely to find several examples of such books in the reference section of any academic library.

This glossary focuses on terms that refer to kinds of evidence to be found in literary texts. It does not include terms that distinguish literary genres or that specify the concepts that are key to different theories of literary analysis.

Simply noting the existence of different sorts of evidence and using the terms does not, by itself, produce a satisfactory essay. An essay must use this evidence to make an argument about the text. The terms are very useful, however, in drawing attention to features of literary texts that might otherwise go unnoticed and in concisely describing features of literary texts that would otherwise require several sentences to specify.

Most of the definitions are followed by Tips for Analysis. The tips may include suggestions for ways to identify certain features of texts, and for ways to begin analyzing those features. A special category of terms refers to formal features of poetry. The Tips for Analysis that follow these terms simply direct you to an earlier section of the book in which the different formal features are discussed together.

Abstract and Concrete

"Abstract" and "concrete" are terms used to describe kinds of language. Abstract language refers to mental constructs such as ideas, feelings, and beliefs. Concrete language, in contrast, refers to objects that can be held, felt, seen, heard, or smelled. "Love," "racism," "justice," and "feudalism" are examples of abstract words. "Kiss," "shoe," and "woman" are more concrete words. A passage or an entire literary text is more or less abstract or concrete depending on the relative balance between abstract and concrete language.

Tips for Analysis: Though creative writers are often advised to favour the concrete over the abstract, in literary criticism the terms are neutral. To state that a passage is abstract or concrete is not to criticize it or praise it. Be aware if the language in a literary text tends to be abstract or concrete. As well, be alert to shifts from one to the other in a single literary text. Such shifts may contribute to meaningful changes in tone, and they may reveal qualities in characters who are being described or who are themselves responsible for the language. Abstract language tends to create a more formal, distant tone, while concrete language is more casual and conversational.

Allegory

An allegory is a literary text in which many of the characters, and in some cases objects, have quite precise equivalents on a second level of meaning. The characters may represent historical figures ("historical allegory") or they may personify abstract qualities ("allegory of ideas"). An example of historical allegory is George Orwell's *Animal Farm*, in which many of the characters represent figures involved in the Russian Revolution. An example of an allegory of ideas is John Bunyan's *Pilgrim's Progress*, in which characters and objects represent elements of the protagonist's spiritual condition; for example, in a famous passage the protagonist falls into "the Slough of Despond," the mud of which represents the doubts that arise in the sinner who is awakened to his spiritual condition.

Tips for Analysis: Be cautious about reading literary texts or passages in literary texts as allegorical. Students can sometimes develop quite elaborate allegorical interpretations that are extremely unconvincing because the evidence to support them is lacking. We generally read literary texts as having a level of meaning beyond what is immediately obvious, but imposing a strict allegorical interpretation on a text can limit rather than expand our understanding. For example, seeing a character as representing a single idea will often lead us to overlook that character's complexity.

Alliteration

Alliteration is the repetition of the consonant sound at the beginning of a series of words. The sound may also occur at the beginning of an accented syllable within a word: "With my grip will I grapple the gruesome fiend."

Tips for Analysis: See Chapter 3: Analyzing the Formal Features of Poetry, pages 34–37.

Allusion

An allusion is a reference in a literary text to another literary text ("literary allusion"), an event in history ("historical allusion"), or, more generally, to anything a culture produces, such as myths, popular songs, works of science, and cartoons. Literary allusions establish a connection between the primary literary text and the one to which the allusion is made. Historical allusions establish a connection between the primary literary text and the historical event alluded to.

Tips for Analysis: Simply noticing when allusions occur can be a challenge, even for experienced critics. It is useful to think about when and in what context the literary text you are studying was written. In certain periods of English literature, for example, by far the most commonly alluded-to text is the Bible. Classical myth is also a rich source of allusion, as is Shakespeare. Some contemporary literature abounds with allusions to popular culture, and younger students may have an advantage over older, more experienced critics when it comes to understanding such texts. Once you identify an allusion, you need to analyze it carefully in order to establish what the relationship is between the primary text and the text or event to which the allusion is made. A literary allusion might suggest that the theme of the primary text is in some way similar to that of the text to which the allusion is made, but it may also be that the meaning of the primary text is emphasized through its contrast to the text alluded to. To be very thorough, you need to have a good understanding of the relevant text or event.

If the literary text you are studying is well known, it may be available in an edition that provides notes that explain its allusions. In the case of longer texts, look for a "critical edition" or simply check different editions in the library to see what notes they provide. Look for shorter texts, such as a single poem, in anthologies that are limited to a literary genre or a national literature. Such anthologies are more likely to have extensive explanatory notes than those that are more general. You may also find helpful notes in collections devoted to a single author.

Aside

An aside is a comment made by a character in a play. It is understood by convention to be heard only by the audience, and not by the other characters on stage. The aside conveys the character's thought.

Assonance

Assonance is the repetition of similar vowel sounds in different words in a single line of a poem, or in words at the ends of different lines in a poem: "a lack of a past."

Tips for Analysis: See Chapter 3: Analyzing the Formal Features of Poetry, pages 34–37.

Blank Verse

Blank verse is unrhymed iambic pentameter (see *Metre*).

Tips for Analysis: See Chapter 3: Analyzing the Formal Features of Poetry, pages 34–37.

Caesura

A caesura is a pause in a line of poetry, whether indicated by a punctuation mark or a space, or simply suggested by syntax: "Here sighs a jar, and there a goose pie talks" (Pope 4.52).

Tips for Analysis: See Chapter 3: Analyzing the Formal Features of Poetry, pages 34–37.

Character

A character is a person presented in a literary text. The main character in a play or narrative is often referred to as the "protagonist."

Tips for Analysis: Students often are drawn to analysis of character, in part because character is interesting to us, but also because we can apply to our analysis the skills we have learned in life. In many literary texts, the characters appear to operate much like real people, and we can analyze their actions and their inner lives just as we would someone we know, based on similar evidence.

It is very important, however, to recognize that characters are not real people but literary creations. Treating characters as real people and the texts in which they appear as psychological case studies leads to unsuccessful literary analysis. It may be useful to begin an analysis of characters with a consideration of elements of their psychologies that would be similar to an analysis of real people, but it is crucial eventually to move to an analysis of how the characters function in the literary text. Always consider how a character contributes to a text's meaning.

It is especially important to recognize when it makes sense to speculate about a character's psychology and when it does not. A consideration of Hamlet's feelings about his mother that draws on Freudian psychology might produce genuine insights; however, it will probably not be productive to speculate about whether a character such as Iago in *Othello* suffers from low self-esteem that might be connected to a poor relationship with his father. In the case of *Hamlet*, Hamlet's relationship with his mother and its place in his motivations are given important attention by the text; the same is not true of Iago and his father. Even in the case of the character of Hamlet, however, a successful interpretation must eventually move beyond psychological analysis to literary analysis; it must consider how the character of Hamlet functions in the play and contributes to its meaning.

Conflict

Conflict is the opposition between two or more forces in a literary text. The most obvious form of conflict is between two characters, but conflict can also occur between characters and their environments, and between opposing needs or desires within a character.

Tips for Analysis: Identifying the category of a conflict ("person vs. person," "person vs. nature," etc.) is not the goal of an analysis. It is, rather, a starting point. The critic must go on to specify the conflict and to consider what it represents. Students frequently have difficulty with internal conflicts. To say that a character is unhappy or afraid is not to identify a conflict. At least two desires, needs, or other factors must be identified and the opposition between them must be clear. For example, if a character desires approval but also seeks independence, then that is a conflict, as the fulfillment of one desire is likely to block fulfillment of the other.

Connotation and Denotation

The most direct sense of a word, its meaning as specified in a dictionary, is its denotation. Its connotation is the meaning it implies less directly, because of the feelings the word evokes and the associations it has.

Tips for Analysis: In many cases, students have little difficulty noticing and analyzing the significance of the connotation of words. Challenges, however, are posed even to experienced critics by literary texts whose contexts are unfamiliar. In such cases, critics should be cautious about assuming that words connote what they do in their own time and culture. Note that the connotation of a word can change, sometimes because of ideas or events that become associated with it. A dictionary that gives the past or historical meanings as well as the current ones, such as the *Oxford English Dictionary*, can be useful.

Consonance

A recurrence of similar-sounding consonant sounds, especially at the ends of adjacent words.

Tip for Analysis: See Chapter 3: Analyzing the Formal Features of Poetry, pages 34–37.

Couplet

A couplet is two end-rhymed lines of poetry.

Tips for Analysis: See Chapter 3: Analyzing the Formal Features of Poetry, pages 34–37.

Diction

Diction is essentially the kinds of words in a literary text. They may be short or long, abstract or concrete, Latinate or Anglo-Saxon, formal or informal, typical of one region or another.

Tips for Analysis: Consider the effect of the diction in a literary text. How does the diction contribute to tone? What does it reveal about the narrator, the speaker, or specific characters? What values or attitudes are implied by the kinds of words used?

Enjambment

Enjambment occurs when one line of poetry is followed by another, with no pause indicated by a punctuation mark or a shift in sense (such as from one clause to another), as in lines three and four of Wallace Stevens's "Anecdote of the Jar": "It made the slovenly wilderness / Surround that hill."

Tips for Analysis: See Chapter 3: Analyzing the Formal Features of Poetry, pages 34–37.

Epiphany

In its religious sense, an epiphany is a manifestation of God in the world. James Joyce used the term in a literary sense, and it has since come into common use to describe a character's moment of heightened awareness.

Tips for Analysis: Avoid using the term to describe any moment in which a character learns something. The heightened awareness does not need to be religious, but it should involve a leap in understanding that expands a character's sense of self or of the world. Consider the significance of what contributes to the epiphany and what its specific content is.

Figurative Language

Figurative language is language used in such a way that it means something different from its usual, dictionary meaning. Specific kinds of figurative language are known as "tropes." Among the main tropes are simile, metaphor, personification, metonymy, and synecdoche.

A simile is a comparison between two things that are unlike each other, frequently using the words "like" or "as." In "The Needle and the Damage Done," Neil Young wrote, "Every junkie's like a setting sun."

A metaphor is a statement that one thing is another thing that it cannot be. In "You're the Top," Cole Porter wrote, "You're the smile on the *Mona Lisa*."

Personification is the attribution of the qualities of a person to something that is not a person. In "Dolor," Theodore Roethke wrote, "I have known the inexorable sadness of pencils" (1).

Metonymy is the use of a word or phrase to refer to something by naming something else with which it is associated. In "The Fiddle and the Drum," Joni Mitchell wrote, "We have all come / to fear the beating of your drum." The beating of the drum refers to the militarism with which it is associated.

Synecdoche is the use of a word or phrase to refer to something by naming one or more of its parts. In Archibald Lampman's poem "June," the speaker says, "through the reeds she ran / urged by the mountain echoes, at her heels / The hot blown cheeks and trampling feet of Pan" (79–81). The "cheeks" and "feet" are parts of Pan, but they are not following by themselves: Pan is following.

Tips for Analysis: Do not confuse a paraphrase of a trope with analysis. Consider what the specific language implies. For example, the statement that "Every junkie is like a setting sun" suggests that everyone addicted to drugs is somehow dying, but the sun is a public symbol of life, and so the simile also implies that the death of a "junkie" is the loss of something invaluable, a life. The simile, by comparing the junkie to the sun, implies an argument against the dehumanizing, and even demonizing, of those who damage themselves with their addictions. It can be useful to note patterns of tropes within a literary text. Throughout Thomas Hardy's novel *The Return of the Native*, for example, the landscape is personified, and critics have taken this pattern to imply the text's valuing of the natural world.

Fixed Forms

Fixed forms are kinds of poetry following traditional patterns of rhyme and metre. The most important fixed form in English literature is the sonnet.

Tips for Analysis: See Chapter 3: Analyzing the Formal Features of Poetry, pages 34–37.

Free Verse

Free Verse is a kind of poetry without a regular metre or rhyme scheme. Usually the line length is also irregular.

Tips for Analysis: See Chapter 3: Analyzing the Formal Features of Poetry, pages 34–37.

Heroic Couplet

A heroic couplet is two lines of end-rhymed iambic pentameter (see *Metre*).

Tips for Analysis: See Chapter 3: Analyzing the Formal Features of Poetry, pages 34–37.

Imagery

Imagery is a very common and sometimes imprecisely used term in literary criticism. There are two main categories of imagery:

1. Figurative Language – An instance of figurative language is an image, whatever the trope (simile, metaphor, and so on).

2. Sensory Description – A description that uses language that refers to qualities that can be sensed directly is an image. Such qualities include colours, elemental flavours (sweet, sour, bitter, etc.), smells, and textures.

Tips for Analysis: Avoid using the terms "imagery" or "image" simply to refer to anything that is concrete; in order to be an image, a passage needs to include figurative language or language that refers to directly sensed qualities. Watch for patterns of imagery and be alert to the connotations of descriptive language. Colours, flavours, smells, and so on frequently have powerful emotional and even moral associations for us.

Irony

There are many kinds of irony, but the two main categories are "verbal irony" and "dramatic irony." A statement is verbally ironic when it conveys something different from or even opposite to its literal meaning. The irony is made apparent by the context of the statement. Dramatic irony occurs when the reader knows more about what is happening in a literary text than characters do; if a character proceeds happily to a meeting that the reader knows will not take place, the situation is dramatically ironic.

Tips for Analysis: It is important to be aware of the potential for verbal irony; to overlook it is to be unaware of possible meanings that are quite different from those conveyed directly or to risk presenting an analysis that will be thoroughly unconvincing to a reader who has recognized the irony. What is suggested by dramatic irony depends on context: the character who knows less than the reader is frequently a figure of fun. It may be, however, that the literary text implies that the limitations of a character's knowledge parallel our own limited understanding of our world.

Metre

Metre is the pattern of stressed and unstressed syllables in poetry. Each unit in the pattern is called a "foot." The following list gives the names of the different kinds of feet (with the noun form followed by the adjective form), the sequence of stressed and unstressed syllables that defines each foot, and an example of the foot in a single word:

iamb/iambic: unstressed, stressed — "beˇlieˊve"

trochee/trochaic: stressed, unstressed — "beˊaveˇr"

spondee/spondaic: stressed, stressed — "theˊreˊfore"

anapest/anapestic: unstressed, unstressed, stressed — "uˇndeˇrstaˊnd"

dactyl/dactylic: stressed, unstressed, unstressed — "beˊauˇtiˇful"

There are also terms that refer to the number of feet in a line:

monometer: one foot

dimeter: two feet

trimeter: three feet

tetrameter: four feet

pentameter: five feet

hexameter: six feet

heptameter: seven feet

The most common metre in English poetry is iambic pentameter.

To mark the metre in a line of poetry is to "scan" the line, and a scanned line is termed a "scansion." Put a forward slash (/) above stressed syllables and a flattened "u" (˘) above unstressed syllables. Mark the end of a foot with a vertical line between words, and mark a pause in the line (see *Caesura*) with a pair of forward slashes (\\) between words.

Tips for Analysis: People pronounce words differently, with different emphases. In England, for example, the second syllable of the word "renaissance" is stressed, while most North American speakers of English will emphasize the first syllable. When scanning poetry, it is important to read it out loud and to mark the beats in a manner that is consistent with the way you speak. For a further discussion, see Chapter 3: Analyzing the Formal Features of Poetry, pages 34–37.

Narrator

In fiction, the narrator is the person telling the story. For a fuller discussion of different kinds of narrators, see *Point of View.*

Onomatopoeia

Onomatopoeia is a word or series of words that imitates in speech the sound to which they refer. The word "splash" is onomatopoeic because it refers to the sound of an object hitting a liquid, and it imitates that sound. Onomatopoeia is a clear example of an important feature of poetry, which is that it establishes a relationship between the sounds of words and their meaning.

Tips for Analysis: See Chapter 3: Analyzing the Formal Features of Poetry, pages 34–37.

Plot

Plot is the sequence of events in a literary text that are connected by cause and effect. A common way to describe plot is to identify a "rising action," which presents a conflict that reaches a "climax," followed by a "falling action" and a "resolution." (See *Conflict*.)

Tips for Analysis: Note that the "resolution" does not mean that the main conflict must be ended; the resolution, in the literary sense, is the text's last comment on the conflict. When analyzing texts in which plot is important—this includes most novels, stories, and plays—it is crucial to analyze the resolution. Avoid the mistake, however, of allowing the structure of the plot to direct the structure of your essay.

Point of View

Point of view refers to the position of the narrator in relation to the story being told. There are two main categories of point of view, "first person" and "third person." In first-person narratives, the narrator is a character in the story, and in third-person narratives, the narrator is not a character in the story.

First-person narrators who draw attention to themselves because of apparent inaccuracies or biases in their observations are called "ironic" or "unreliable" narrators. Those whose reports seem to be accurate are called "reliable." All first-person narrators, however, reveal something about themselves, even those whose accounts are most trustworthy.

Third-person narrators are categorized according to how much they know about the thoughts and feelings of the characters. An "omniscient" narrator has access to the inner life of everyone in the story. Such a narrator may comment on the thoughts of only a few main characters, but the narrator's capacity to see into the characters' minds is clear. The "limited omniscient" narrator knows the inner life of only one character. "Objective" narrators do not know the thoughts of the characters and can comment only on what they observe externally.

Tips for Analysis: All narrators are fictional creations and should not be confused with the author, even in unusual cases when the narrator has the author's name. The things that a narrator says count as evidence that the critic needs to analyze, even when the narrator comments directly about meaning, or states what the theme is.

Note that to say that a first-person narrator is ironic or unreliable is not to criticize the character; it is a neutral observation about what the narrator reveals. Remember that first-person narrators can be reliable about some things and unreliable about others. Most critics, for example, believe that the narrator of Charlotte Perkins Gilman's "The Yellow Wallpaper" is relatively reliable when describing her husband, but they take her to be unreliable when describing the wallpaper. Be alert to the potential for a narrator's reliability to shift over the course of a narrative. The narrator of Ken Kesey's *One Flew over the Cuckoo's Nest,* for example, becomes increasingly reliable.

Limited omniscient narratives can raise issues of reliability similar to those of first-person narratives. The narrator can report things as though they are filtered through the consciousness of the main character (another term for limited omniscience is "central consciousness"). The narrator may even use the vocabulary and manner of expression of the main character. It can be easy to make serious errors if this potential is overlooked. A third-person narrator might, for example, use racist language that ironically reflects on the main character, in which case we must recognize that the main character's consciousness is controlling the way the narrator reports events.

Although objective narrators do not comment directly on what characters think or feel, they do reveal characters' inner lives. Be attentive to the way that objective narrators dramatize characters' thoughts and emotions by describing their gestures, their facial expressions, their speech, and so on. Note, also, that the term "objective" does not mean that the story itself is neutral toward its actions or characters.

Rhyme

Rhyme is the repetition of the sound of words, or the sound of syllables at the ends of words, including vowels and concluding consonant sounds. Rhymes frequently occur at the ends of lines of verse ("end rhyme") but also within lines ("internal rhyme").

A pattern of end rhyme is a "rhyme scheme." Rhyme schemes are marked with lowercase letters at the ends of lines. Place the letter "a" after the first line. Place another "a" after the next line if it rhymes with the first, to indicate an end rhyme. If the sound is not repeated, place a "b" at the end of the second line. Continue this process through the poem. Each new rhyme is indicated with the next letter in the alphabet, and each repeated rhyme is marked with the letter that corresponds to its sound. The following example gives the rhyme scheme for the first eight lines of Shakespeare's "Sonnet 3":

Look in thy glass and tell the face thou viewest (a)

Now is the time that face should form another (b)

Whose fresh repair if now thou not renewest (a)

Thou dost beguile the world, unbless some mother (b)

For where is she so fair whose uneared womb (c)

Disdains the tillage of thy husbandry? (d)

Or who is he so fond will be the tomb (c)

Of his self-love, to stop posterity? (d)

Thus "viewest" and "renewest" are both marked "a" because they rhyme; any line that rhymed with them would again be marked "a." "Another," at the end of the second line, is a new sound, so it is marked "b," and so is any line that rhymes with it.

Tips for Analysis: See Chapter 3: Analyzing the Formal Features of Poetry, pages 34–37.

Setting

The setting is the physical and historical place in which the action of a literary text occurs. It may be a single room, a region or nation, a specific day, an era, and so on.

Tips for Analysis: The physical setting can contribute to the mood of a literary text, and changes in setting may emphasize shifts in mood and meaning. The physical setting has the potential to be symbolic, and when it is described in detail critics should be particularly attentive to its significance. Setting in drama and film, sometimes called "*mise en scène*," is often crucial. Pay close attention to the stage directions describing the lighting, props, and scenery, or, in film, to camera angles, lighting, and other features of cinematography. The historical setting of a text is obviously important when considering the significance of the historical context.

Soliloquy

A soliloquy is a speech given by an actor in a drama, usually while alone on stage. By convention, the speech is understood to express what the character is thinking.

Sonnet

A sonnet is a fixed form of poetry comprising fourteen lines of rhymed iambic pentameter. "Petrarchan" (sometimes called "Italian") sonnets follow the rhyme scheme abbaabbacdccdc or abbaabbacdecde. "Shakespearean" (sometimes called "English") sonnets follow the rhyme scheme ababcdcdefefgg. A connected series of sonnets is a "sonnet cycle."

Tips for Analysis: Since early in the twentieth century, some poets have experimented with sonnets that vary the traditional rhyme scheme and break up lines. Such poems are still considered to be sonnets. For a further discussion, see Chapter 3: Analyzing the Formal Features of Poetry, pages 34–37.

Speaker

The speaker is the person to whom we attribute the words of a poem. The term is used rather than "narrator" to reflect the oral nature of poetry.

Tips for Analysis: Do not confuse the speaker with the author. With some poems, it is clear that the speaker is a character, different from the author, but even when the poem does not present us with such a speaker, the distinction still holds. A poem may appear to be autobiographical, but we do not read it as biography. It is a literary text, and the characteristics of the speaker are to be discovered by evidence in the text, not through identifying the speaker with the author.

Stanza

A stanza is a group of lines forming a section of a poem, usually set off by a space between it and other sections. The lines in the stanza have a similar metre, and they frequently rhyme. Stanzas have names that correspond to the number of lines they contain or to their metre and rhyme scheme:

couplet: two lines

tercet or triplet: three lines

quatrain: four lines

rime royal: seven lines of iambic pentameter, with the rhyme scheme ababbcc

ottava rima: eight lines, with the rhyme scheme abababcc

Spenserian stanza: nine lines, the first eight of which are iambic pentameter, the last iambic hexameter, with the rhyme scheme ababbcbcc.

Tips for Analysis: See Chapter 3: Analyzing the Formal Features of Poetry, pages 34–37.

Style

The style of a work includes anything that distinguishes its language. It can include diction, patterns of figurative language, syntax, sentence length, and so on.

Tips for Analysis: Students frequently overlook style when analyzing literary texts. When revising your essays, consider how an analysis of some element of style can support your argument. Note that style can shift, and that such shifts may be linked to changes in characters, in mood and tone, or in the attitude of a speaker or narrator. Student work that includes even a brief discussion of the significance of style in a literary text can stand out as admirably ambitious.

Symbol

A symbol is a concrete thing that represents something else, usually something more abstract. Symbols can be divided into two broad categories, private and public.

A private symbol is one whose meaning is established by the literary text in which it appears. For example, the essay in this book that analyzes Wallace Stevens's poem "Anecdote of the Jar" treats the jar as a symbol of human creation. Jars do not have such symbolic meaning generally; the symbolic meaning is created by the poem.

A public symbol is one whose meaning is widely known by a large group of people, without relying on the literary text to establish that meaning. Many such symbols come from religion. To a reader with even a passing acquaintance with Christianity, for example, the symbolic meaning of a cross will be clear without any emphasis from the literary text in which it appears. (For a reader with no background in Christianity, some research would be necessary to discover that the cross is a symbol of Christianity itself, and, more specifically, of Jesus Christ.)

Tips for Analysis: It is sometimes difficult to know when something in a literary text should be treated as a private symbol. Notice when special attention is directed to something in a text. Our attention can be drawn by titles, by detailed descriptions of objects or scenes (especially when they have little connection to the plot), by the way characters in a text respond to an object, and by unusual language, especially figurative language, being used to describe something.

Public symbols also present difficulties. You might not be a member of the group in which something is widely recognized as a symbol. It is important to pay attention to the relevant cultural contexts of a text you are analyzing and to be prepared to do some research if you are not familiar with those contexts. That research can be as simple as asking someone more familiar with the background of a text whether they recognize something as a symbol, and what its meaning might be.

When you say that one thing symbolizes something else, make sure that the relationship is clearly a symbolic one and not something else. Students sometimes say one thing symbolizes something else when it can more properly be considered an example of something or as revealing something. If a character takes a drink of water, it is probably more useful to think of that action as revealing that the character is thirsty rather than as symbolizing thirst. A pen is not a symbol of a writing instrument; it is an example of a writing instrument. On the other hand, it might be established in a literary text as a symbol of something related to its function, such as communication or learning, or it might even be established as a symbol of something entirely unrelated to its use.

Syntax

Syntax is the order of words and clauses in sentences.

Tips for Analysis: Note when the syntax in a text is unusual, and consider what the effect is. Unusual syntax may call attention to a character in a text and reveal something about him or her. It may also create a certain tone. Consider, for example, the following two sentences:

1. Which shelf did you put the book on?
2. On which shelf did you put the book?

There is no significant difference in the diction of these sentences, yet there is a contrast in tone that has to do with a difference in syntax. The second sentence is ordered in such a way that it does not end with the preposition "on." Such a syntax creates a more formal tone than the first sentence does.

Theme

A theme is an idea about the world, expressed by a literary text, of general importance to people.

Tips for Analysis: For a full discussion of theme, see Chapter 3.

Tone

The tone of a literary text is similar to the mood that it establishes. It can also be thought of as the attitude of the work toward its subject matter. A text can be humorous in tone, or angry, sorrowful, regretful, nostalgic, and so on.

Tips for Analysis: It is important that tone not be overlooked, especially when it is particularly marked. An analysis that fails to note the tone of a text that is obviously comic or passionately angry will fail to be convincing.

Trope

A trope is a specific type of figurative language, such as simile, metaphor, metonymy, etc.

Tips for Analysis: See the entry for Figurative Language.

Verse Paragraph

A verse paragraph is a section of a poem marked by spaces between it and other sections. It differs from a stanza in that it is not part of a pattern of sections having the same length and unified by metre or rhyme. Sections of free verse poems are verse paragraphs, not stanzas.

Tips for Analysis: See Chapter 3: Analyzing the Formal Features of Poetry, pages 34–37.

STRUCTURE AND MECHANICS MARKING ABBREVIATIONS

\\ TITLES

T   The title needs revision. See Chapter 4: Titles, page 54.

\\ INTRODUCTORY PARAGRAPHS

I/Op   The opening to the introductory paragraph is missing one or more elements. See Chapter 4: Introductory Paragraphs, page 48.

I/EP   The evidence preview is missing or needs revision. See Chapter 4: Introductory Paragraphs, page 48.

I/L   The link from the evidence to the theme is missing or needs revision. See Chapter 4: Introductory Paragraphs, page 48.

\\ THESIS STATEMENTS

Th/C   The statement of theme needs to be connected to a literary text. See Chapter 3: Effective Statements of Theme, page 38.

Th/N   The statement of theme applies only to the literary text or to too narrow a group. See Chapter 3: Effective Statements of Theme, page 39.

Th/T   The statement of theme identifies only a topic. See Chapter 3: Effective Statements of Theme, page 39.

Th/I   The statement of theme needs to identify a more important idea. See Chapter 3: Effective Statements of Theme, pages 39–40.

Th/PP The statement of theme pluralizes the plot. See Chapter 3: Effective Statements of Theme, page 40.

Th/EP The statement of theme empties the plot. See Chapter 3: Effective Statements of Theme, page 41.

Th/Ne The statement of theme makes the text seem neutral. See Chapter 3: Effective Statements of Theme, page 40.

Th/R   The statement of theme reduces the idea the text expresses to a simple moral. See Chapter 3: Effective Statements of Theme, page 39.

Th/K   The statement of theme should include key words from the abstract topic. See Chapter 4: Introductory Paragraphs, page 49.

\\ ANALYTICAL PARAGRAPHS

A/C   The paragraph needs to begin with a claim about the literary text. See Chapter 2: Claims, pages 8–9.

A/C/K   The claim should repeat key words in the thesis. See Chapter 4: Sample Outline: Logical Sequence Structure—Literary Analysis, page 45.

A/E   Evidence to support the claim needs to be presented immediately after the claim. See Chapter 2: Evidence, page 11.

A/R   The analysis needs to refer directly to the evidence. See Chapter 2: Analysis, page 13.

A/Ex   The analysis needs to explain more carefully how the evidence does what you say it does and supports the claim. See Chapter 2: Analysis, pages 12–13.

A/K   The analysis needs to repeat key words from the claim. See Chapter 2: Analysis, page 13.

A/Th   The wording of the final claim should be close to that of the thesis. See Chapter 4: The Difference between a Logical Sequence and a List, page 45.

\\ INTEGRATING QUOTATIONS

IQ/S   The quotation must be integrated into a sentence of your own. See Chapter 2: Integrating Quotations from Literary Texts, page 20.

IQ/W   You must make clear whose words are being quoted. See Chapter 2: Integrating Quotations from Literary Texts, page 21.

IQ/I   More information must be presented so the reader can understand the quotation. See Chapter 2: Integrating Quotations from Literary Texts, page 21.

IQ/P   Refer to the quotation in the present tense. See Chapter 2: Integrating Quotations from Literary Texts, pages 21–22.

IQ/En   The introduction to the quotation needs to refer to the entire quotation. See Chapter 2: Integrating Quotations from Literary Texts, page 22.

IQ/V   The verb referring to the quotation is not accurate. See Chapter 2: Integrating Quotations from Literary Texts, page 22.

IQ/SG   The sentence containing the quotation is not grammatically or syntactically correct. See Chapter 2: Integrating Quotations from Literary Texts, page 22.

IQ/Su   Do not use a quotation as the subject of a sentence. See Chapter 2: Integrating Quotations from Literary Texts, page 23.

WORKS CITED

The Bible. Introduction and notes by Robert Carroll and Stephen Prickett. Authorized King James Version, Oxford UP, 1998.

Bunyan, John. *The Pilgrim's Progress.* 1678–84. Edited by Cynthia Wall, Norton, 2008.

Callahan, David. *Rainforest Narratives: The Work of Janette Turner Hospital.* U of Queensland P, 2009.

Camus, Albert. "The Guest." 1957. Translated by Justin O'Brien. *The Story and Its Writer: An Introduction to Short Fiction,* edited by Ann Charters, Bedford/St. Martin's, 1987, pp. 211–20.

Carver, Raymond. "The Bridle." 1982. Moffett and McElheny, pp. 343–60.

Dickstein, Morris. *Gates of Eden: American Culture in the Sixties.* 1977 ed., Penguin, 1989.

Erdrich, Louise. "Scales." Moffett and McElheny, pp. 229–38.

Greenblatt, Stephen, editor. *The Norton Anthology of English Literature: Major Authors.* 8th ed., Norton, 2006.

Hardy, Thomas. *The Return of the Native.* 1878. Modern Library, 2001.

Heller, Joseph. *Something Happened.* Knopf, 1974.

Highway, Tomson. *The Rez Sisters.* Fifth House, 1988.

Houle, Karen. "During, Three." *During.* Gaspereau, 2008, pp. 13–14.

Kesey, Ken. *One Flew over the Cuckoo's Nest.* Signet, 1963.

Kilmer, Joyce. "Trees." *Complete Poems.* Buccaneer, 1998, p. 180.

Lampman, Archibald. "June." *Lyrics of Earth.* Copeland and Day, 1895, pp. 78–79.

Mitchell, Joni. "The Fiddle and the Drum." *Clouds,* Reprise, 1969.

Moffett, James, and Kenneth R. McElheny, editors. *Points of View: An Anthology of Short Stories.* Penguin, 1995.

Orwell, George. *Nineteen Eighty-Four*. 1948. S. J. Reginald Saunders, 1949.

Partridge, Elise. "Farewell Desires." *Chameleon Hours*, Anansi, 2008.

Pope, Alexander. "The Rape of the Lock." 1712. Greenblatt, pp. 1138–55.

Porter, Cole. "You're the Top." *Anything Goes*. Harms, 1936.

Roethke, Theodore. "Dolor." 1948. *The Collected Poems of Theodore Roethke*, Doubleday, 1966, p. 44.

Shakespeare, William. *Hamlet*. 1623. Edited by Harold Jenkins, Methuen, 1982.

———. *Othello*. 1623. Edited by Ernst Anselm Joachim Honigmann, Methuen, 2001.

———. "Sonnet 3." 1609. Greenblatt, p. 498.

Stevens, Wallace. "Anecdote of the Jar." 1923. *The Collected Poems: The Corrected Edition*, edited by Chris Beyers and John N. Serio, Vintage International, 2015, p. 81.

Williams, William Carlos. "The Red Wheelbarrow." *The Collected Poems, Volume 1, 1909–1939*, edited by Arthur Walton Litz and Christopher MacGowan, New Directions, 1938, p. 224.

Wyatt, Thomas. "Whoso list to hunt." 1557. Greenblatt, p. 350.

Young, Neil. "The Needle and the Damage Done." *Harvest*, Reprise, 1972.

INDEX